The Dreaded Thirteenth Tennessee Union Cavalry

Marauding Mountain Men

Melanie Storie

Published by The History Press
Charleston, SC 29403
www.historypress.net

Copyright © 2013 by Melanie Storie
All rights reserved

First published 2013

Manufactured in the United States

ISBN 978.1.62619.112.9

Library of Congress CIP data applied for.

Notice: The information in this book is true and complete to the best of our knowledge. It is offered without guarantee on the part of the author or The History Press. The author and The History Press disclaim all liability in connection with the use of this book.

All rights reserved. No part of this book may be reproduced or transmitted in any form whatsoever without prior written permission from the publisher except in the case of brief quotations embodied in critical articles and reviews.

To the memory of my dad, Charles William "Bill" Greer, whose ancestors bravely served with the Thirteenth Tennessee Union Cavalry.

Contents

Preface	7
Acknowledgements	9
Introduction	11
1. "A Civil War Among Us"	17
2. "Rally 'Round the Flag"	45
3. "You Have Killed the Best Man in the Southern Confederacy"	61
4. "A Night of Horror"	71
5. Stoneman's "Cossacks"	83
6. "Such Are the Fortunes of War"	105
7. "Their Glory Shall Not Be Blotted Out"	117
Notes	135
Index	149
About the Author	159

Preface

The research and writing for this work began many years ago. The journey started quite innocently as a genealogical project when I was a college undergraduate history major. Growing up in Southwest Virginia, I did not know much about my father's family except that that they were from Western North Carolina and family tradition held that his grandfather was an orphan raised by an aunt and uncle. Eventually, I discovered that several members of my paternal ancestors fought in the Civil War and had served with a volunteer Union cavalry regiment from East Tennessee. This in itself made me extremely curious. North Carolina and Tennessee were both part of the Confederacy, so what made these men choose to fight for the Union? Also, since they were from North Carolina, why did they join a regiment from East Tennessee? And so it went. The more anecdotes I found, the more interested I became.

Very little exists in the way of primary sources about the Thirteenth Tennessee Volunteer Union Cavalry. Virtually no letters or diaries written by the soldiers have survived, and very few original photographs still exist. So when I stumbled upon a series of reunion photographs taken in the late nineteenth and early twentieth centuries, I was ecstatic. The owner discovered them in her aunt's attic and had posted them to the Internet with the hopes that someone would recognize the veterans. Thus, I began scouring local newspapers from the late nineteenth century for any scrap of information about the veterans' reunions. Among the sparse and torn newspaper copies of the *Elizabethton Mountaineer*, I finally found

Preface

Private James R. Allen was the son of Wesley Allen, a carpenter in Johnson County, Tennessee. Young James enlisted with Company D in 1863; he was only fifteen years old. Allen survived the war and worked as a farmer in Johnson County until his death in 1923. *Courtesy of Tony Marion.*

an article from 1896 detailing the very first reunion held by the Thirteenth Tennessee Cavalry Association in Butler, Tennessee. Also the regimental history written by Samuel Scott and Samuel Angel, published in 1903, provided vital clues in my search for information. As veteran officers from the Thirteenth Tennessee, their book supplied details of wartime events, albeit with a touch of bias, as is evident in most Civil War regimental accounts published at the same time.

The research has taken me on many journeys from archives to cemeteries. Along the way, a narrative began to take shape as different threads created a story—more than just a military history but one filled with personal hardships, loss and sacrifice. For instance, the story of Mary Miller Head, whose husband, Private Daniel S. Head, died a prisoner of war in the notorious Andersonville prison camp in Georgia. She was left a widow with four children to raise, the youngest only four months old. Likewise, service records revealed letters from soldiers requesting leave in order to take care of families left behind enemy lines in East Tennessee. Yet the capstone for the project came in making the acquaintance of a private collector who had in his possession unpublished photographs of soldiers from the Thirteenth Tennessee. Being able to look into the face of fifteen-year-old James R. Allen, who lied about his age in order to serve his country, inspired me to finish this project.

Acknowledgements

There are many individuals who share in this publication. First I would like to thank The History Press and their willingness to help me make a longtime project a reality. In particular, I would like to thank J. Banks Smither, who worked with me from day one and was a great help in guiding me through the process. I am appreciative of my colleagues in the Department of History at East Tennessee State University. Over the years, there have been several members of this department, too many to name specifically, who have served as wonderful mentors to me. Thank you to all those individuals who scanned photographs for me at the Tennessee State Library and Archives, the Georgetown Library Special Collections Research Center, the U.S. Army Heritage and Education Center, the New-York Historical Society and the East Tennessee Historical Society. To the descendants of Thirteenth Tennessee soldiers, thank you so much for sharing your photographs and letters. In particular, I would like to thank Cheryl Clark, Joyce M. Schellenger, Jud Scott and Tom Ward. A big thank-you to Professor Allen Ellis, descendant of famed Civil War pilot Daniel Ellis, for his willingness to share information and ultimately putting me in contact with Tony Marion, private collector and historian. Tony Marion and his wife, Betty, were so gracious to open their beautiful, historic home to me. They made me feel right at home, and I cannot express enough thanks to them for allowing me to come and look at the photographic collection. Prior to this publication, many of the photographs of the Thirteenth Tennessee soldiers in Tony Marion's collection have never before been published. They add a wonderful flavor to the book.

It is safe to say that without the support and encouragement from my family, this book would not exist. I was blessed with two wonderful parents who invested much love, time and energy into teaching my brother and me the true values of life. My biggest fan and greatest friend is my mom, Louise Greer. Thank you for your unconditional love and unlimited faith in my ability to do whatever I set my mind to. One of my greatest regrets is that my dad did not live to see this publication, particularly since he provided the inspiration behind the idea that became this book. This work is dedicated with love to his memory. I am equally blessed to have the best "little" brother in the world, Chuck Greer. While we picked on each other as kids and drove our parents crazy, we share many wonderful childhood memories that I would not trade for anything. To my children, Josh and Emilee, you both make me very proud to be your mom. I love you more than you will ever know. To my husband, Bill, we've shared a wonderful journey together for over two decades, and I'm looking forward to many more years together. You are the love of my life and the anchor that holds me steady. Thank you for all of your patience, love and constant encouragement. Also, your contributions in editing the manuscript were invaluable. Finally, all that I am or ever hope to be is due to the saving grace of Jesus Christ—"I can do all things through Christ who strengthens me." (Philippians 4:13)

Introduction

During the late 1960s and early 1970s, Dr. Thomas Burton and Dr. Ambrose Manning, both English professors at East Tennessee State University, received a grant to conduct an oral history project. Their numerous recordings captured such things as old-time mountain musical performances, folk stories and accounts of everyday life from residents primarily of Western North Carolina. During one interview from the 1960s with Mr. Thomas Guy of Watauga County, North Carolina, there was talk about the hardships of the Civil War and specifically the impact of Union general George Stoneman's raid on the area during the last days of the war. Mr. Guy was born about 1889 and therefore had no direct memories of the war, but he recounted specific stories told to him by his grandfather, Marion Milsaps, who had served in the Confederate army. In the interview, Mr. Guy related that as Stoneman marched his men through Western North Carolina, the Thirteenth Tennessee Volunteer Cavalry accompanied him. He made a point to the interviewers that the Thirteenth Tennessee had a reputation for brutality, and as "these mean bunch of men" marched through the region "they shot all the home guards they could find."[1] Confederate Tennesseans held Unionist Tennessee soldiers in contempt, labeling them "home Yankees." More despicable than Northern soldiers because they had seemingly betrayed their state and their people, "home Yankees" became targets at which Confederate Tennesseans took special aim, believing they were not fit to live among civilized Southerners. One Confederate Tennessean described "home Yankees" as "the roughest most

Introduction

good-for-nothing men who would not join the Confederates but waited for an opportunity to join the Federals that they might stay near home and pilfer the houses in the community as well as settle their grudges by attacking their personal enemies."[2]

As a result of the bitter feelings, many "home Yankees" believed they too had a score to settle for the hardships endured at the hands of Confederate soldiers and sympathizers. Captain H.K. Weand, of the Fifteenth Pennsylvania Cavalry, who fought alongside Unionist East Tennesseans, wrote that these men held such animosity because they "had suffered terrible cruelties at the hands of the rebels. They had been hunted and shot down as unworthy of any humanity." In return for their loyalty to the Federal government, many had lost loved ones, their homes and all their worldly possessions. Thus, when the "tables were turned and disloyal families were at their mercy, they repaid what they had suffered."[3] Loyalty displayed by many East Tennesseans during the Civil War had roots that reached back many generations prior to the conflict.

The area known as East Tennessee spans from the Cumberland Mountains on the west to the Unaka Mountains on the east. It is one of the three grand divisions of the state of Tennessee. East Tennessee, for the most part, is a mountainous region with wooded hills, rich valleys and a temperate climate. The early settlements were established along the Watauga, Nolichucky and Holston Rivers.[4] Historically, East Tennesseans are known for rugged individualism. Before the American Revolution, settlers came looking for better opportunities for themselves and their families. In his book *The Winning of the West*, Theodore Roosevelt described East Tennesseans as "a sturdy race, enterprising and intelligent."[5] They survived Indian attacks, war and the wilderness. They possessed a sense of order and the need for the rule of law. Thus, when settlers crossed over the mountains into what later became East Tennessee, they established the first representative government west of the Appalachians, called the Watauga Association. Under this written constitution, a "committee of thirteen" was elected to serve as the general legislative body. They held court to compose laws and manage the settlements. Judgment was quick and final with no appeal process.[6]

During the first years of the American Revolution, East Tennessee settlements were not directly affected. Yet by 1780, the war had shifted southward, and as the war spilled into the southern backcountry, settlers faced a threat to their homes. British major Patrick Ferguson sent word to the "backwater men," as he called them, demanding they immediately stop supporting the American cause and acknowledge British authority. Ferguson concluded this message with a threat to "march over the mountains, hang their leaders, and lay their country to waste with fire and sword" if the settlers refused to comply. This served only to rouse the settlers into action, and over one thousand volunteers from East Tennessee, Virginia and North Carolina gathered at Sycamore Shoals in Carter County, Tennessee, on September 25, 1780, to prepare to defend their homes and land. Once mustered into service, the men marched over the mountains into North Carolina and met up with Ferguson and his Loyalist army at Kings Mountain, on the North Carolina–South Carolina border. The Overmoutain Men, as they came to be called, not only inflicted a thundering defeat on the enemy but also killed Ferguson in the process.[7] The victory at Kings Mountain coupled with winning American independence instilled a great wave of patriotism and national loyalty in East Tennesseans, as well as in the generations to come.

In the years preceding the Civil War, East Tennessee developed differently from Middle and West Tennessee both socially and politically. While slavery existed in East Tennessee, the region did not support large cash-crop plantations as in other parts of the state. In 1860, the statewide slave population numbered approximately 270,000. Of this number, only 10 percent of slaves lived in East Tennessee counties.[8] Unlike Middle and West Tennessee, which generally supported the Democratic Party, East Tennessee tended to side with the Whig Party. Leery of an aristocratic planter class that dominated the Democratic Party, many East Tennesseans joined the Whig Party in the 1840s because of a promise of federal aid for internal improvements. During the 1860 presidential election, the Whigs had long disappeared as a formal political party, but some of their ideas remained. Voters of East Tennessee therefore cast ballots for the Constitutional Union Party, a party that contained many Whig elements. At a time when the other political parties had taken a decided stance on the issue of slavery, the Constitutional Union Party adopted a platform that simply stated its support for the Constitution as the law of the land and its support for preservation of the Union. It neither condemned nor expressed support for the institution of slavery. John Bell, Middle Tennessean and a former Whig, headed the party's presidential ticket in 1860. Bell carried only three states—Virginia, Kentucky and Tennessee—and did not garner more than 50 percent of the popular vote in any state. Ironically, within a year of the election, John Bell and many other moderates of the Constitutional Union Party pledged their support to the Confederacy.[9]

As Tennessee ran headlong in support of secession, Unionists in East Tennessee called conventions to stop the process. While they failed in the

Introduction

attempt to halt secession, overall East Tennessee refused to support the Confederacy. Notable Unionist leaders like Thomas A.R. Nelson, Horace Maynard, Oliver P. Temple, Andrew Johnson and William G. "Parson" Brownlow all contributed to the rhetoric, which clearly influenced East Tennesseans in their support of the Union.[10] Once secession was a reality, Unionists worked from within East Tennessee to strike at the Confederate war machine. They burned bridges and cut vital communication and supply lines. To stop the treasonous acts, the Confederacy imposed martial law and arrested Unionists. This prompted many men to travel through enemy lines in order to volunteer with the Union army. It is estimated that East Tennessee alone furnished over thirty thousand volunteers for the Union army. Beginning in 1863, Unionists formed their own distinctive units, one of which was the Thirteenth Tennessee Volunteer Cavalry. The commissioning of this regiment resulted largely from the efforts of Congressman Roderick R. Butler, state representative for Carter and Johnson Counties. Through his influence coupled with the lobbying of the Federal government by Andrew Johnson and Horace Maynard, the regiment was mustered into service under the command of Colonel John K. Miller.[11]

Called the "Loyal Thirteenth," the men came primarily from the counties of upper East Tennessee and Western North Carolina.[12] Because of this, most of the events discussed in this work focus primarily on those counties. More than 1,400 men came to serve with the Thirteenth Tennessee. Their ranks consisted of mainly farmers, but there were also millworkers, carpenters, shoemakers, teachers, doctors, ministers, students and lawyers. Along with native East Tennesseans, there were at least three Irishmen and over twenty African Americans who made up their ranks. The average enlistment age was twenty-five; however, this may be somewhat misleading since regimental historians Samuel Scott and Samuel Angel recorded that at least two hundred soldiers were under the age of eighteen, some as young as fifteen. Since the age requirement was eighteen for military service, underage recruits reported their age as eighteen to the mustering officer when, in fact, they were much younger. Most had never traveled more than a few miles from their homes, but by the end of the war, they had marched over three thousand miles, passing through six different states.[13]

The student of the Civil War will not find the Thirteenth Tennessee Volunteer Cavalry listed among the regiments that participated in the well-known battles of Shiloh, Antietam, Vicksburg or Gettysburg. Nevertheless, the service provided by the men of the Thirteenth Tennessee was equally important. The men were amateur soldiers, but they learned quickly and preformed bravely when led by example. There were, however, some serious breaches in discipline, which often coincided with poor leadership. General Edward McCook remarked after the war, "God bless your old East Tennessee souls, don't you know your loyalty and devotion gave us of the North the courage to fight, when everything looked like darkness of despair? I can't say that their discipline was perfect, but their fighting was."[14]

Most of the young men who joined the Thirteenth Tennessee had never fired a gun at another human being. So when civil war erupted across the nation, life in rural East Tennessee changed dramatically. Families were split over loyalties either to the United States or to the Confederate States. For many of the families in upper East Tennessee, the focus of this study, loyalties fell to the Union side, but there were pockets of support for the Confederacy. Because the number of slaves and slave owners in the region was very low, it appeared that the issue of slavery by itself did not factor much into the reasons for an individual's loyalty. However, that is not to suggest that loyal citizens of East Tennessee supported the abolition of slavery. Indeed, some of the most outspoken Unionists, such as Andrew Johnson, Horace Maynard, William B. Carter and Thomas A.R. Nelson, were also slave owners. In fact, after President Abraham Lincoln issued the Emancipation Proclamation, Unionism in East Tennessee cooled considerably. For instance, Nelson responded to emancipation saying, "If I had believed it was the object of the North to subjugate the South and to emancipate our slaves in violation of the Constitution, I would have gone as far as the farthest in advocating resistance to the utmost extent…the Union men [of] East Tennessee are not now and never were Abolitionists."[15]

Men from upper East Tennessee from the counties of Washington, Carter, Sullivan, Hawkins, Johnson and Greene risked their lives early in the war to make their way through enemy lines into Kentucky, where they could join the Union army. To say the least, life was deplorable for those loyal East Tennesseans who remained under Confederate occupation. Many young boys, too young to enlist in 1861, witnessed and experienced atrocities inflicted on their families and homes at the hands of brutal Confederate home guards. By the time the Thirteenth Tennessee Volunteer Cavalry was organized in the fall of 1863, many of these boys were old enough (or believed they were) to enlist and had a burning desire to settle the score. Because they were not trained soldiers, the idea of military discipline was a foreign concept, and sometimes emotion won out over duty and honor. At times, some of the men took part in shameful activities such as terrorizing slaves who gathered in contraband camps, looting homes of Confederate

Introduction

sympathizers and destroying communities in retribution for injustices suffered by East Tennesseans. This caused some Union leaders like General Richard Johnson to complain that some of the Tennessee cavalry regiments were just as bad as the enemy guerrillas they were fighting. Yet when led by competent men, the regiment could fight well. For instance, in the spring of 1864, U.S. cavalryman William H. Ingerton, not a West Pointer but nonetheless an experienced career soldier, arrived at a decisive time to help bring proficiency to the Thirteenth Tennessee. He drilled and imposed military discipline as they had never before experienced. This training proved vital when the regiment surprised and defeated General John Hunt Morgan, one of the most celebrated Confederate cavalry commanders, at Greeneville, Tennessee, during the fall of 1864. The fight cost Morgan his life and catapulted the Thirteenth Tennessee into widespread acclaim for the Union but established a reputation of notoriety from the Confederacy. The glory quickly faded, however, as the regiment suffered setbacks and losses in the latter part of the year. By 1865, the last year of the war, it was clear that the Thirteenth Tennessee would be used not to fight battles but inflict chaos, pain and suffering to drive the Confederacy to its knees. Many never made it back home; some died in action, more perished from disease, while still others wasted away in Confederate prison camps. For those who did survive, the experience of war remained with them the rest of their lives. While their wartime participation was often ruthless, the postwar years revealed veterans of the Thirteenth Tennessee wanted to leave behind a legacy of honor for their descendants. This is their story.

Chapter 1

"A Civil War Among Us"

In 1860, fourteen-year-old John G. Burchfield was living in Carter County in the small, rural community of Elizabethton, situated in upper East Tennessee. Like many young boys of the day, politics did not generally occupy his thoughts much. He was too busy helping on the family farm, fishing with his friends and working as a blacksmith's apprentice. Yet little did he realize how much his life would change over the course of the next four years. Not only did young Burchfield become immersed within a Unionist protest movement, but he also became one of the young soldiers who later joined the Thirteenth Tennessee Volunteer Cavalry.

With the election of Abraham Lincoln in November 1860, seven states from the lower South passed ordinances of secession and formed the Confederate States of America. In February 1861, Tennessee governor Isham Harris and the state legislature called for a special referendum on whether to call a state convention to consider secession. Tennessee voters went to the polls on February 25 and rejected the call for a convention on secession by a margin of 69,357 to 56,535. In East Tennessee, the vote was much more lopsided, with 33,299 voting against a convention to 7,070 who favored holding one.[16]

Nevertheless, events quickly conspired to change the views of many Tennesseans on the issue of secession. On April 12, 1861, the first shots of the Civil War rang out over Fort Sumter in South Carolina's Charleston Harbor, prompting President Lincoln a few days later to call on the states for seventy-five thousand volunteers. Interpreting this as a threat to the South, the Southern

The Dreaded Thirteenth Tennessee Union Cavalry

Isham Harris served as Tennessee's governor from 1857 to 1862. A West Tennessean, Governor Harris was a staunch secessionist and successfully led the state out of the Union. Once the Union army gained control of Nashville in 1862, President Abraham Lincoln appointed Andrew Johnson as military governor of Tennessee. Harris spent the rest of the war as an aide to various Confederate generals. After the war, he fled to Mexico and then to England for a time before returning to Tennessee and being elected a U.S. senator in 1877. He held this position until his death in 1897. *Courtesy of the Library of Congress.*

states of Virginia, Arkansas and North Carolina joined the Confederacy.[17] Ironically, John Burchfield witnessed these events in Charleston, as he and his father had driven some hogs down from East Tennessee. As a young boy, he commented that he "was impressed with the portent of the storm."[18] The news of Fort Sumter and Lincoln's call for troops to suppress the rebellion arrived in East Tennessee before the Burchfields returned. Having witnessed the events unfold in Charleston, young John became much more aware of the serious political climate. Therefore, the implications of Governor Harris's response to President Lincoln's call for volunteers were not lost on the young man or on the tens of thousands of Tennesseans. In a communication to the White House, Harris declared, "Tennessee will not furnish a single man for the purposes of coercion, but 50,000 if necessary, for the defense of our rights and those of our Southern brothers."[19]

In the weeks that followed, both secessionists and Unionists launched intensive public speaking campaigns. Men such as Thomas A.R. Nelson, Connally Trigg, Horace Maynard, Andrew Johnson, Oliver Temple and John Baxter campaigned throughout East Tennessee giving speeches in favor of the Union. Notable men such as Landon C. Haynes, William H. Sneed, William Cocke, William G. Swan, Joseph B. Heiskell and others undertook support for the Confederacy in East Tennessee. In Elizabethton, a debate was planned between the two groups. A platform was placed near the courthouse, where Joseph Heiskell of Rogersville and William Cocke of Knoxville were billed to speak on behalf of secession. Reverend William B. Carter and Nathaniel G. Taylor, both from Carter County, were selected to defend Unionism. Reportedly, thousands from Carter and surrounding counties turned out for the public debate. From the beginning, however, the mood was contentious, with many in the audience carrying pistols. At one point, the debate became personal as the Carter family lineage was called into question. No doubt that caused an audible gasp, since the Carters were among the first settlers to the area and very influential. In fact, the county itself was named in honor of William Carter's grandfather. Some in the audience were notably jumpy, as was made evident when a young lady tossed a bouquet of flowers onto the platform showing her appreciation for the speakers. Some men immediately jumped to their feet with pistols drawn. Nevertheless, the event concluded peacefully.[20]

About two weeks following the public debate in Elizabethton, David Kitzmiller, a Baptist minister and outspoken secessionist from Johnson County, penned a letter to Governor Harris. Writing on behalf of the county's secessionist element, Kitzmiller sought to provide the governor with "some of the practical operations of Unionism" in the county. Complaining that the "conduct of the Union party is too intolerable to be borne," Kitzmiller claimed Unionists were "threatening the lives of the secessionists" without reason. Estimating that Union men in Carter and Johnson Counties outnumbered secessionists at least nine to one, the reverend pleaded for protection from the governor, affirming, "Secessionists will have to leave here or submit, you have no idea what we have to endure." Unionists, he claimed, were in direct communication with President Lincoln and were making plans to fight for the Union if the state seceded. The leading Unionist agitator, in Kitzmiller's opinion, was Congressman Roderick Butler. Butler's conduct, he wrote, "has not a parallel in the south," as he constantly encouraged East Tennesseans to vote against secession. Kitzmiller openly worried that unless something changed there would be "a civil war among us here." Fearful that Unionists might discover his letter, Kitzmiller wrote, "I will have to mail this letter in Virginia to keep down suspicion."[21]

Many in upper East Tennessee received their mail and local news via stagecoach. On April 18, a stagecoach carrying the mail and a few passengers arrived in Johnson County, Tennessee, from Abingdon, Virginia, some thirty miles away. Two of the men on the stagecoach were from Virginia, and they checked into a Taylorsville hotel owned by Samuel Northington. That evening, the men caused a commotion in the street by shouting and waving a Confederate flag in loud celebration of the recent secession of Virginia. Northington, a Unionist, cautioned them that Tennessee had not seceded and many townspeople did not support the Southern Confederacy. The men took offense and replied they had a right to celebrate and furthermore did not care what Unionists thought. That evening, Northington, along with his son Hector and fellow Unionist Joseph Wagner, agreed they would take the flag, by force if necessary, if the men displayed it again. The next morning, as the Virginians emerged from their rooms, they prepared to ride through town waving the Confederate flag. As they mounted their horses, the three Unionists appeared with shotguns and demanded the flag be handed over. One of the men began to swear at the elder Northington and challenged him to try to take it. To that end, Northington began shooting several holes in the flag. Caught off guard, the men handed over what was left of the flag and quickly rode out of town.[22] Realizing the seriousness of their position, the people of Johnson County on April 27 assembled at the courthouse to declare their "attachment for the Union and the Constitution of our Fathers." Further, they contended there was no "just cause for a disruption of this government." The resolutions asserted the people of Johnson County wanted to live in peace and were willing "to be passive spectators." Other East Tennessee counties followed the same example with similar statements.[23]

In early May, Governor Harris called for a second referendum to gain approval of an "Ordinance of Secession." After voters defeated a call for a secession convention earlier in the year, the governor sought to bypass the step altogether and put secession to a direct vote without a convention. In the meantime, Harris took steps that aligned Tennessee in a military league with the Confederacy. Outraged, Unionists called for their own convention to address what they labeled the governor's unconstitutional and pro-secessionist actions. A two-day convention took place at Temperance Hall in Knoxville on May 30–31. Over four hundred delegates representing twenty-eight counties attended. Thomas A.R. Nelson of Washington County was appointed president. Nelson spoke for an hour, during which time he denounced the state government's pro-secession actions as unconstitutional. The delegation then drafted a list of grievances and resolutions. U.S. senator Andrew Johnson was also in attendance and spoke for nearly three hours. He further condemned the state government's disregard for the U.S. Constitution and claimed leadership had fallen prey to "fanaticism." It was resolved by the delegates that the governor did not have the authority to enter into a military league with the Confederacy. The meeting adjourned, but before leaving, delegates planned to meet again in the very near future.[24]

On June 8, Unionists suffered a devastating defeat as Tennessee voters approved an ordinance of secession by a vote of 101,486 to 46,520, thereby giving the state government power to sever its ties with the United States and join the Confederacy. East Tennessee voters had opposed the ordinance by a 32,205 to 14,095 margin.[25] While Tennessee had officially seceded, many East Tennessee Unionists were determined to be a thorn in the side of the Confederate government.

Nelson called for a second convention of Unionists to be held in Greeneville, Tennessee, on June 17. During the four-day meeting, there were lengthy debates as to what action could be taken by East Tennessee. After much deliberation, a series of resolutions was passed. These resolutions expressed that East Tennessee desired to remain neutral in the coming war; that the legislature's acts of declaring Tennessee independence and joining a military league were unconstitutional; that East Tennessee would defend itself if occupied by Confederate forces and would retaliate if any delegates were harmed. Delegates also formed a commission to travel to Nashville in order to seek permission from the legislature to form a separate state from the eastern counties. They agreed that even if statehood was rejected by the legislature, East Tennesseans held the right to determine their own destiny. Finally, a "Declaration of Grievances" was adopted proclaiming that East Tennessee would remain within the Union, affirming that the Lincoln administration had given them no reason to secede.[26]

The memorial requesting that East Tennessee be separated from the state of Tennessee was largely ignored by the state legislature. The Confederacy could not, and would not, allow such an essential area to break away. The region provided a vital transportation and communications link, as well as great resources in the way of food, livestock and minerals. Connecting rail lines of the East Tennessee and Virginia (ET&V) and East Tennessee and Georgia (ET&G) Railroads passed through the great valley from Bristol to Chattanooga. The Confederacy needed these rail lines to transport troops and materials to military theaters in the East and South. Additionally, East Tennessee held great value in wheat production and was also an important source of raw materials like copper, lead and saltpeter. To lose this area not only would create serious logistical problems but would also open an avenue of invasion by the Union army into the heartland of the Confederacy.[27]

East Tennessee Unionists nevertheless were bitter about the legislative snub of separation. As a result, some began to leave the area, as they were

The Dreaded Thirteenth Tennessee Union Cavalry

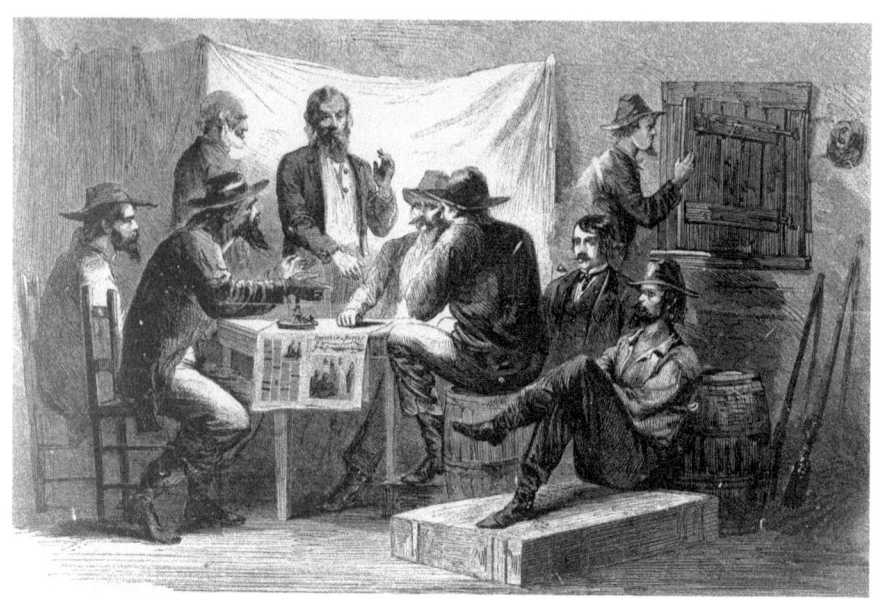

Secret Meeting of Southern Unionists as sketched by Civil War artist Alfred R. Waud and appeared in *Harper's Weekly* on August 4, 1866. After Tennessee seceded and joined the Confederate States of America, many Unionists met in secret to plot sabotage against the Confederacy or to discuss plans for crossing the mountains into Kentucky to join the Union army. *Courtesy of the Library of Congress.*

unwilling to live under Confederate occupation. Others traveled to Kentucky in order to join the Union army. Yet many other Unionists remained unyielding and were determined to fight for their homes. Some began laying plans of sabotage aimed at Confederate war efforts, while still others planned to raise their own military forces to engage in guerrilla warfare. Joseph Wagner, who had helped Samuel Northington disarm secessionists in Johnson County, began recruiting forces. He was elected colonel of the county militia and enrolled nearly 250 men. Eventually, Wagner would be commissioned a major with the Thirteenth Tennessee Volunteer Cavalry and his men added to the muster rolls.[28]

To defend the region against any invasion Union forces might launch, Confederate leadership assigned General Felix K. Zollicoffer to command the Confederate District of East Tennessee. A native of Middle Tennessee, Zollicoffer had no formal military training except for a brief stint in the army during the Seminole War in Florida during the 1830s. Before the war, Zollicoffer had worked primarily as a newspaper editor. Historians have often criticized him for being an incompetent political general, but to be fair, he was placed in an untenable position. Faced with communication and supply problems that the mountainous region of East Tennessee presented, Zollicoffer had to maintain the longest line of defense for the Confederacy with a small number of poorly armed men. Not to mention his command encompassed an area that contained the least amount of support for the Confederacy and the greatest amount of Unionist activity.[29]

Interestingly, Zollicoffer did not support the early secessionist movement in Tennessee. He did not believe the election of Abraham Lincoln constituted such a threat that necessitated dissolving the Union. Yet when fighting erupted at Fort Sumter and Lincoln called for troops to use against the South, Zollicoffer, along with many other Tennesseans, abandoned support for the Union cause. He now believed that all Tennesseans, without regard to any former attachment to the Federal Union, should support the Confederacy. His orders from Adjutant and Inspector General Samuel Cooper were to "preserve peace, protect the railroad, and repel invasion."[30] After establishing his headquarters at Knoxville, Zollicoffer dispatched troops to prepare the defenses against a Northern invasion. He reasoned that the best way to deal with Unionists was through leniency. To that end, he issued a proclamation addressed "To the People of East Tennessee" in August 1861. He firmly declared that treason against the state "will not be tolerated" but then reassured citizens that "no man's rights, property, or privileges shall be disturbed." Zollicoffer explained the military was there only to protect the people from invasion and to prevent "the horrors of civil war." Further, he appealed to the "Union men" not to be swept up in any excitement so as to bring destruction to their fellow Tennesseans.[31]

Yet the Confederate government remained alarmed, with good reason, about the possibility of sabotaging the vital communication and railroad bridges on the ET&V and ET&G lines. Individuals such as Roderick Butler and Samuel Northington were singled out by Zollicoffer as potential troublemakers, and he ordered that these men, along with other so-called Lincolnites in East Tennessee, be placed under close observation. Zollicoffer continued that he wanted "as much as possible to be conciliatory"; however, if "satisfactory evidence" was obtained that these men or others like them were promoting "open hostility to the authorities of the State and of the Confederate States," they should be arrested and detained.[32] In a letter to Confederate secretary of war Leroy P. Walker, Governor Harris openly expressed his concerns, saying, "There will be an effort on the part of the Federal Government to arm the Union men of Tennessee I have no doubt." Because of the threat the Union element posed for Harris, he indicated that his government would "have to adopt a decided and energetic policy with the people of that section."[33] Confederate senator and Carter County native Landon C. Haynes echoed the same apprehension in a dispatch to President Jefferson Davis. Warning of the danger East Tennessee Unionists posed, Haynes wrote, "It is a grand mistake to suppose the Union party in East Tennessee has lost its hostility to the Confederacy." He forewarned that unless the spirit of rebellion was crushed, "the railroads will be destroyed, the bridges burned and others will follow."[34] As it turned out, Haynes's fears were realized, and the policy of clemency was abandoned as the loyalists of East Tennessee took drastic steps against the Confederacy during the fall of 1861.

Despite promises of leniency from Zollicoffer, Unionists were at work developing a plan designed to strike a blow at the Confederacy. William Carter had given speeches in support of the Union and served as a delegate to the Greeneville Convention, yet since the time of Tennessee's secession the Presbyterian minister had developed a plan of sabotage. Carter believed the loyalist population could effectively cripple the Confederacy if they acted quickly. He secretly slipped through enemy lines to Kentucky, where his older brother Samuel P. Carter, a U.S. Naval Academy graduate and soon-to-be brigadier general, was enlisting fellow East Tennesseans into service. Before the war, Samuel Carter was serving as a lieutenant with the navy but was recalled with the outbreak of hostilities. Their younger brother, James P.T. Carter, was also busy in Kentucky raising a regiment made up of East Tennessee refugees. Later, he would become colonel of the Second East Tennessee Mounted Infantry. William Carter continued on to Washington, D.C., where he gained an audience with Union

William Blount Carter (circa 1850), Presbyterian minister and Unionist, helped orchestrate the November 1861 bridge burnings in East Tennessee. He was a member of the prominent Carter family of Elizabethton. *Courtesy of the East Tennessee Historical Society, Knoxville, TN.*

leadership. In a meeting with President Abraham Lincoln, Secretary of State William Seward and General George B. McClellan, Carter presented the details of the plan that called for the destruction of nine vital railroad bridges along a 270-mile span from Bristol, Tennessee, to Bridgeport, Alabama. A crucial element of the plot was to have the Union army amassed on the Kentucky-Tennessee border ready to invade once the bridges were destroyed. Lincoln approved the plan and allocated $2,500 with which to fund the operation.[35]

In his letters to General George H. Thomas, commander of the Federal troops in Kentucky, Carter related that East Tennessee "is in a wretched condition; a perfect despotism reigns here," but the "Union men of East Tennessee are longing and praying for the hour when they can break their fetters." He avowed they remained "firm and unwavering in their devotion to the government and anxious to have an opportunity to assist in saving it."[36]

Carter finalized plans and assigned men to the task of burning each of the bridges. All the bridges would be burned at the same hour on the night of November 8, 1861. The operation was so clandestine that for many years following the incident, the names of those involved were closely guarded.[37] Daniel Stover of Elizabethton, Andrew Johnson's son-in-law, was commissioned a colonel and assigned to burn the Watauga River Bridge at Carter's Depot and the Holston River Bridge at

Colonel Daniel Stover, a son-in-law of Andrew Johnson, was recruited by Reverend William B. Carter to help coordinate burning the bridges in November 1861. He organized the Fourth Tennessee Infantry during the spring of 1863, and it was composed of men from East Tennessee. Unfortunately, he became ill soon after and died in December 1864. *Courtesy of the Tennessee State Library and Archives, Nashville, TN.*

Union Depot. Stover assembled a group of loyal men into a company called the East Tennessee Bridge Burners. Many of these same men would later play an active role in the war with the Thirteenth Tennessee Volunteer Cavalry.[38]

In the Watauga River Bridge vicinity, an area called Turkeytown, Colonel Stover enlisted help from Samuel A. Cunningham, who was T.A.R. Nelson's son-in-law; Andrew D. Taylor; Harrison Hendrix; and his nineteen-year-old son Solomon H. Hendrix. Stover sent young Hendrix to observe Confederate activities and troop strength at the bridge. Getting to the bridge was somewhat difficult, as recent heavy rain had caused the Watauga River to become very swollen. Therefore, when Hendrix tried to cross the river at Taylor's Ford, he was assisted by William Taylor, one of Andrew Taylor's slaves. While he was a slaveholder, Andrew Taylor was a Unionist. Later, when news of emancipation reached East Tennessee, William Taylor joined the ranks of the Thirteenth Tennessee as a cook. Hendrix made his observations and reported to Stover that the bridge was heavily guarded by a detachment of 120 Confederate soldiers under the command of Captain David McClellan.[39]

Meanwhile, Stover approached George W. Emmert, also a resident of Turkeytown, and assigned him to report on the Holston River Bridge at

Lieutenant George W. Emmert was involved early on in Unionist efforts in Carter County. He reported on Confederate troop strength at the Holston River Bridge at Union Depot. After the bridge was burned in November 1861, Emmert was arrested but later released. He and several other men from the county hid in the mountains until they mustered into service with the Thirteenth Tennessee. During the war, Emmert suffered a gunshot wound to the abdomen. He survived the war and returned to Carter County, where he worked as a farmer and engaged in the mercantile business. He died in 1918 at the age of eighty-nine. *From Scott and Angel*, History of the Thirteenth Regiment, *facing 176.*

Union Depot. Emmert took the train from Carter's Depot to Bristol, Tennessee, and purposely missed the return train that evening. He wanted to be able to walk back through the town of Union and make his observations about bridge security. Emmert learned from Mr. Hazy Davis, a Unionist and resident living near the bridge, that only two men routinely guarded the bridge. After receiving the reconnaissance reports about both bridges, Stover decided that because the Carter's Depot Bridge was so heavily guarded, it could not be burned. Although according to a claim made by Dr. Abraham Jobe, a Carter County Unionist, in his autobiography, he approached Colonel Stover and convinced him not to burn the Watauga River Bridge because he worried about retaliation from the Confederacy if the Union army failed to invade after the bridges were destroyed.[40]

While the bridge at Carter's Depot survived, the Unionists torched the Holston River Bridge at Union Depot. John Burchfield participated in the bridge burning that evening. Because of his young age, Stover did not directly recruit Burchfield. In fact, it was mainly due to the young man's curious observations that he learned of the planned sabotage. He had been hanging around with some other boys near Lafayette Cameron's store in Elizabethton when he witnessed an intense meeting taking place in the storeroom. As Burchfield walked into the room, he recognized many men from town and noticed the very determined looks on their faces. When the men noticed him, he was firmly told to leave. Not fully aware of the subject being discussed, Burchfield's curiosity only intensified when William Gourley approached him at John J. Eden's blacksmith shop. This was the shop where Burchfield apprenticed, and Gourley instructed the boy to have a mare ready for him that evening. Not one to let an adventure pass him by, Burchfield readied a horse not only for Gourley but one for himself as well. Later that evening, he slipped out of his room and waited at Eden's place, where several other men including William Gourley soon gathered. As they rode together, Gourley offered a sobering statement, saying, "Boys, we have a dangerous job on [our] hands tonight. It will be death to any of us should we be captured." The gravity of this charge remained with Burchfield all his life.

When the men arrived at the Holston River Bridge, the two guards, Stanford Jenkins and William Jones, were taken by surprise. When Jones saw the men, he immediately turned and ran away. From the group of saboteurs, John Burrow raised his gun to shoot Jones, but fearing the sound of the shot would raise an alarm, Burrow was ordered to hold his fire. The other Confederate guard surrendered and immediately began to beg for mercy. Many of the men were concerned about the escape of Jones, but more

Ruins of the Holston River Bridge, located in the town of Bluff City, Tennessee. *Author's collection.*

Ruins of the Holston River Bridge, Bluff City, Tennessee. *Author's collection.*

Train mural painted in recent times on some of the Holston River Bridge ruins in Bluff City, Tennessee. *Author's collection.*

immediately they debated as to what should be done with Jenkins, since he had recognized nearly all of them. It was quickly decided they first must take care of burning the bridge and then determine Jenkins's fate. Pine knots and turpentine were used to help burn the bridge quickly. Once it was in flames and the men were safely away, a discussion began about what to do with Jenkins. Some wanted to kill him since he could identify them, but others such as Jonas Keen argued against killing him and instead contended to let him go. Jenkins, who at one time had worked on Keen's farm, promised faithfully if his life were spared he would not betray them as the bridge burners. After swearing an oath, Jenkins was released. Of the nine bridges targeted, only five were destroyed. While the bridge at Carter's Depot was not destroyed, the telegraph lines were cut.[41]

The morning after the bridges were set ablaze, news spread quickly of the sabotage. Reports poured into the Confederate high command detailing the damages inflicted by Unionists. Panic was evident when William F. Moore, justice of the peace from Washington County, Virginia, wrote to Virginia governor John Letcher. Moore reported that a conductor of the ET&V Railroad had confirmed the Holston River Bridge at Union Depot had been destroyed and telegraph lines cut. Further, he reported that the bridge at Carter's Station was in danger of being destroyed as a large Unionist force, reportedly as many as five hundred, was massing for an attack. Given the

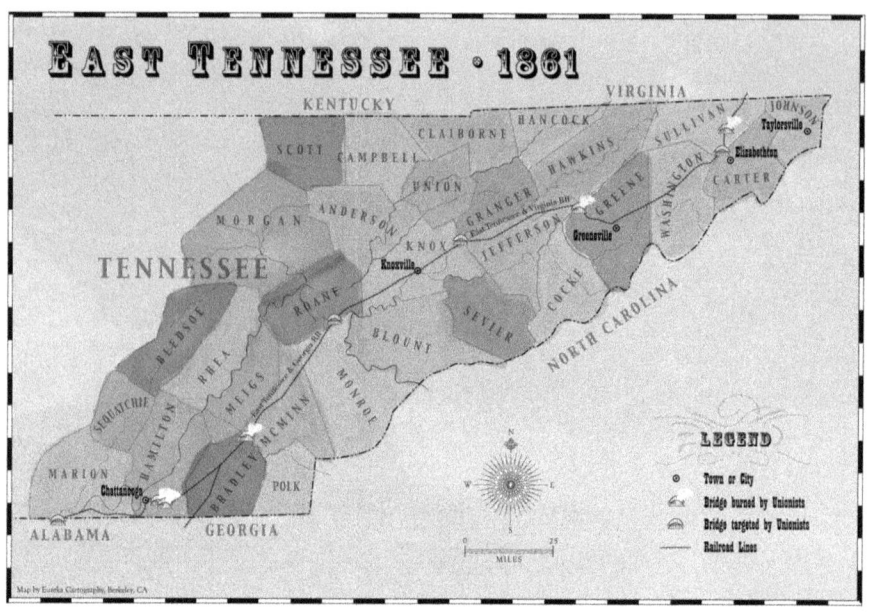

Artist's rendition of East Tennessee Bridge burning in 1861. *Courtesy of Eureka Cartography.*

serious situation, Moore asked the governor to appeal to President Davis to call out the militia to suppress the rebellion in East Tennessee. Additionally, John R. Branner, president of the ET&V Railroad, sent word to newly installed Confederate secretary of war Judah P. Benjamin about bridges being destroyed and communications interrupted. He expressed a fear that unless the government took swift military action, Unionists would "destroy or take possession of the whole line from Bristol to Chattanooga."[42] Both Unionists and Confederates believed the Union army was now marching toward East Tennessee; little did they know that the plan had changed.

In Kentucky, General William T. Sherman, commander of the Department of Ohio, had developed a case of cold feet. Writing from Louisville, Kentucky, the day before the bridge-burning operations were set to take place, Sherman confided to General Thomas that while the expedition into East Tennessee no doubt was important, he did not believe they had "force enough and transportation to undertake it."[43] Thomas, in preparation of the invasion, had moved with his army from Camp Dick Robinson toward the Tennessee border when Sherman ordered him back. With one swift blow, Sherman had called off the invasion, and now it was too late to notify the Unionists of the change in plans.

As far as the Unionists were concerned, they had taken the step in rebellion, and the Federal army was on its way to support their efforts. Loyalists from all across upper East Tennessee gathered in Elizabethton. Well over 1,000 men had assembled at Nathaniel Taylor's farm, determined to hold firm against Captain McClellan's Confederate detachment now moving from Carter's Depot to suppress the rebellion. Branner continued to make reports to Secretary Benjamin, confirming, "Lincolnites are forming an encampment at Elizabethton," gathering "1,000 to 1,300 men and more coming within six miles of our railroad at Watauga bridge." The bridge had survived the initial attacks, but Branner was concerned it could still be destroyed. Additionally, he worried about the bridge near Strawberry Plains, which had also survived the night, but he feared Union forces might "burn the bridge and take possession of the road." If these two bridges were destroyed then all transportation through East Tennessee would be halted. Further, he continued that Unionists were "cutting telegraph lines as quickly" as they were put up. After a brief skirmish later called the Carter County rebellion, Captain McClellan withdrew his troops. However, Benjamin assured Branner that more Confederate troops were on their way to "crush the traitors."[44]

As East Tennesseans continued to wait for the Union army to appear on the horizon, Andrew Johnson pressed the necessity of invasion with General Thomas, to which Thomas replied he had done everything within his power to secure the necessary troops and transportation to go into East Tennessee. He affirmed, "I can only say that I am doing the best I can. Our commanding general is doing the same, and using all of his influence to equip a force for the rescue of Tennessee." While Thomas was sympathetic to the predicament of East Tennesseans and their quest "to relieve their friends and families from the terrible oppression," he recognized that an invasion was doomed to fail since Union forces were unprepared. Thomas already acknowledged that a successful campaign into East Tennessee required at least four additional regiments. Likewise, Johnson was becoming a nuisance to Thomas as he wrote, "It is time that discontented persons should be silenced both in and out of the service."[45]

On November 1, General George McClellan became general-in-chief of all the Union armies, replacing the retiring Winfield Scott. McClellan soon afterward replaced General Sherman with General Don Carlos Buell as commander of the Department of Ohio. Buell was a close friend of McClellan, and after making the change, McClellan explained to Buell the importance of supporting East Tennessee. McClellan wrote, "A large majority of the inhabitants of Eastern Tennessee are in favor of the Union," and he maintained that Buell should sustain a strong defensive line in order to "enable the loyal citizens of Eastern Tennessee to rise."[46] Both Andrew Johnson and Horace Maynard wrote to Buell, "Our people are being oppressed and pursued as beasts of the forest; the Government must come to their relief."[47] However, Buell did not seem to attach the same priority to East Tennessee and looked to strike the Confederate armies at Bowling Green and Nashville.

After a long and perilous journey, William Carter on November 16 arrived at Camp Calvert, Kentucky, with the latest report about the bridge-burning mission. His brother, Brigadier General Samuel Carter, immediately dispatched a message to General Thomas. In his message, General Carter reported that his brother's forces had "succeeded in having burned at least six, and perhaps eight, bridges on the railroad." He reiterated, "The Union men are waiting with longing and anxiety for the appearance of Federal forces…and are all ready to rise up in defense of the Federal Government." General Carter reminded Thomas of the importance of such an invasion and urged him to "advance into East Tennessee; now is the time."[48]

Despite the calls to send an invading force into East Tennessee, both Thomas and Buell stalled. Clearly, this delay caused President Lincoln a great deal of anxiety. In a letter to General Buell on January 4, 1862, Lincoln wrote, "Have arms gone forward for East Tennessee?" Buell replied that the arms could only go forward under protection of an army and at the moment "preparations have been delayed far beyond my expectations and are still incomplete." McClellan also wrote to Buell about the necessity of a "speedy occupation of East Tennessee" and that he regretted to hear that Buell did not consider an invasion top priority. Buell quickly tried to explain to McClellan that his response to the president had been misunderstood and that he considered East Tennessee "of the highest importance." Nevertheless, the inaction by Buell caused Lincoln to express a worry that "our friends in East Tennessee are being hanged and driven to despair."[49] Lincoln's fears were well founded because as the Union delayed, the Confederate government took swift action against the bridge burners.

Without the support of the Union army, the lives of loyal East Tennesseans were in certain peril. The Confederate government demanded the traitors be severely dealt with in order to make an example of them. Governor Harris reported to Jefferson Davis, "The burning of the railroad bridges in East Tennessee shows a deep-seated spirit of rebellion in that section. Union men are organizing. The rebellion must be crushed out instantly, the leaders arrested and summarily punished."[50] In response, Davis's government immediately imposed martial law and arrested Unionists. Secretary of War Benjamin ordered that the "traitors in East Tennessee" were to be "tried summarily by drum-head court-martial and if found guilty executed on the spot by hanging." He added, "It would be well to leave their bodies hanging in the vicinity of the burned bridges."[51] Anyone else considered disloyal to the Confederacy would be arrested and treated as a prisoner of war. They were to be sent to the military prison in Tuscaloosa, Alabama, until the end of the war or until they took an oath of allegiance. Confederate colonel Danville Ledbetter was assigned the task of protecting the railroads between Bristol and Chattanooga, as well as hunting down the culprits and punishing them. Colonel Ledbetter, after assessing the situation, reported to General Albert S. Johnston that despite the "disturbed condition" of East Tennessee, he promised the bridges would be rebuilt and communication lines repaired. He also noted that Unionist forces were gathering all across the region. Apparently, some expected Andrew Johnson to make an appearance in his hometown of Greeneville. Ledbetter wrote that his friends were "disappointed." Ledbetter proposed to General Johnston that he would "move against them at the earliest possible moment."[52] After receiving his orders, Ledbetter immediately issued a proclamation to the citizens of East Tennessee in which he warned, "You are citizens of Tennessee and your State is one of the Confederate States. All men taken in arms against the Government will be transported to military prison."[53]

Instead of liberation, the destruction of the bridges brought persecution to East Tennesseans. The Confederacy, making good on the threat of prosecution, quickly assembled military tribunals in Greeneville and Knoxville in order to convict and execute several bridge burners. Jacob M. Hensie and Henry Fry were the first two to face execution for bridge burning in connection with the Lick Creek Bridge near Greeneville. Their trial and execution took place on the same day. William Brownlow claimed that Colonel Ledbetter "tied the knots with his own hands," and men were hanged from a tree north of the railroad depot in Greeneville. As per Benjamin's orders, their bodies were left hanging, in full sight of the trains that passed, for four days and nights before being removed. Passengers could use canes and sticks to strike the dead bodies from the train's rear platform as they passed. Also convicted for the Lick Creek Bridge burning were Alex C. Haun, Harrison Self and Jacob Harmon and his sixteen-year-old son Thomas. Haun and both Harmon men were executed in Knoxville in December 1861. Within hours of Harrison Self's execution, Jefferson

The Dreaded Thirteenth Tennessee Union Cavalry

An engraving depicting the way in which bridge burners Henry Fry and Jacob Hensie were hanged and their bodies left by the railroad. *From William G. Brownlow's* Sketches of the Rise, Progress, and Decline of Secession; with a Narrative of Personal Adventures Among the Rebels, *301.*

Davis granted him a pardon, largely due to the pleading of Self's daughter Elizabeth. Benjamin, obviously pleased with the progress to crush the Unionists' rebellion, wrote to Confederate district attorney John C. Ramsey: "I am very glad to hear of action of the military authorities and hope to hear they have hung every bridge-burner at the end of the burned bridge."[54]

Confederate sympathizers, still in the minority in many East Tennessee counties, saw a chance for revenge by assisting authorities in identifying those Unionist men they considered traitors. General Zollicoffer observed, "Citizens have turned out in large numbers and assisted the soldiers in scouring the mountains and hunting down the fugitive traitors." Once an advocate for leniency, Zollicoffer declared that Unionists "should now be pursed to extermination if possible."[55] Madison T. Peoples, a Carter County lawyer and Confederate sympathizer, wrote to Secretary Benjamin saying, "In my judgment there is not a Union man in Carter County who was not involved to some extent in the rebellion." Being a lawyer, Peoples recommended, "Martial law ought to be enforced in every county in East Tennessee to hold these bad men in proper restraint."[56] Stanford Jenkins, the Confederate guard whose life was spared at the Union Depot Bridge, wasted no time in reporting the identities of the bridge burners. George Emmert and Solomon Hendrix, who had supplied vital information to Colonel Stover about the bridges, were some of the first to be arrested in Carter County. It seems, however, that neither man was ever tried or punished in connection with the bridge burning. Family members of Hendrix provided him with an alibi for the time of the bridge burning, forcing Captain McClellan to release him under house arrest. Upon release, Hendrix sent a warning to other Unionists that their identities had been revealed to the Confederate authorities.[57]

Writing from Kentucky, Lieutenant Leonidas C. Houk, of the First Tennessee, expressed the frustrations many East Tennessean soldiers felt about the situation facing their families back home. He related to Andrew Johnson that those East Tennessee refugees who made it to Kentucky were "of the impression that the government is either a failure, or it cares nothing for the East Tennesseans." He also shared news from East Tennessee, writing, "The Bridge burning business has brought upon the people, the fiery vengeance of the Rebel horde! They are redoubling their diligence in the work of Treason, and Tyrannical oppression! Arrests, and punishment… have become common—the Secessionists are running to and fro, over the country!" Houk lamented to Johnson, "Will the government do nothing to emancipate Such heroes, and patriots, as the East Tennesseans, have proven to be?…My good Sir, it does Seem cruel to leave those Brave people to the tender mercies of those who have proved to be Incarnate Devils…Oh! my God, how long until East Tennessee will be redeemed?"[58]

As a prominent state representative, Roderick Butler did his best to defend Unionists who had been arrested. He was born in Wytheville, Virginia, on April 2, 1827, to George and Nancy Anne Leitch Butler. George Butler died before his son was barely a year old. Roderick, at the age of thirteen, became a tailor's apprentice and later moved to Johnson County, Tennessee. He studied law and was admitted to the board in 1853. Aligning himself with the Whig Party, Butler became a judge and was later elected as a Republican to the Tennessee General Assembly in 1859.[59] Butler remained with the state legislature even though Tennessee voted in favor of secession. Governor Harris informed members of the legislature they must take an oath to the Confederacy or be sent to prison. A committee of Union men formed in protest. Senator Samuel Pickens, who represented Cocke, Sevier, Blount and Greene Counties, resisted taking the oath to the Confederacy. As a result, he was arrested and sent to prison in Tuscaloosa, Alabama, where he later died.

The other Union men decided to take the oath in order to keep the Union element together and to protect their Unionist constituents.[60]

After several men from Carter County, in November 1861, were arrested and transported to Nashville for trial, Butler used his influence to gain their release. Among those arrested was Hamilton C. Smith, who was charged with making incendiary speeches against the Confederacy. The other prisoners were charged with bridge burning. Smith recalled that Butler met the train at the Nashville depot and came to the car in which they were being held. When they appeared in court before Judge West Hughes Humphreys, Butler was there to defend them against the charges. Appointed to the Confederate District Court of Tennessee by Jefferson Davis, Humphreys was formally a U.S. district judge who was impeached for supporting secession. Eventually, the court agreed to release Smith on a $20,000 bond, which Butler secured for him. After Smith was released, Butler furnished him with a suit of clothes and took care of all his expenses. The next few days were spent in talking about the oppression of and the cruelty shown to the Union men of East Tennessee at the hands of the Confederacy. When Smith was ready to return to his home in East Tennessee, Butler paid for the ticket.

For the other men accused of bridge burning, Butler worked to have them released as well. David Taylor remembered that Butler visited him and the others while in jail and brought them such things as tobacco and bread. The prisoners had other visitors too. Confederate enlistment officers routinely visited the jail offering release to any prisoner willing to join the Confederate army. Worried the men might join the Confederacy due to weariness of prison conditions, Butler used some inventive, if not comical, ways to convince Judge Humphreys to release the men. Such was the case of Alfred Gourley, a forty-seven-year-old laborer from Carter County charged with bridge burning. When Butler came to visit, he whispered to Gourley to act "as if he was a lunatic" when he appeared before Judge Humphreys. In court, Gourley professed to have no sense and appeared to walk with a severe limp. The judge agreed to release him into Butler's custody.[61]

To avoid imprisonment altogether, many Unionists sought refuge in the mountains or concealed themselves near their homes so as not to be discovered. Men such as Daniel Stover, Daniel Ellis, Jonas Keen, G.O. Collins and other bridge burners hid out in the Pond Mountains in the eastern part of Carter County. They stayed well away from any settlements and became dependent on other Unionists to help supply them. They constructed temporary shelters and shanties and spent weeks waiting for news of the Union army's arrival.[62] Others, like Dr. Jobe, took refuge in their cellars to avoid arrest. For six weeks, the physician found himself a prisoner in his own home, fearing imprisonment or death if he emerged. His wife successfully hid him while spreading the rumor that her husband had fled to the mountains. An elaborate system of signals was developed to let Jobe know when Confederate troops were present. One of the house servants would go into the kitchen and begin rocking the baby's cradle, which covered the door leading to the cellar, and sing lullabies to cover any noise made from the cellar. At other times, certain family members' names were spoken to alert Jobe when it was all clear or when the soldiers were around the home. After six weeks, Jobe emerged from the cellar, but his life was often in jeopardy from marauding groups of Confederate soldiers.[63] Thus, by the end of 1861, as Unionists were arrested or went into hiding, it appeared the rebellion in East Tennessee had been crushed. Colonel Ledbetter reported, "It is believed that we are making progress toward pacification. The Union men are taking the oath in pretty large numbers and arms are beginning to be brought in…The execution of the bridge-burners is producing the happiest effect…I trust that we have secured the outward obedience of the people."[64]

With the Confederate crackdown on Unionists and no sign of the Federal army to assist the loyal population in East Tennessee, a network emerged that served to guide military recruits into Kentucky. Individuals who guided the men were known as "pilots," and they took great personal risk in the face of imprisonment or death for their traitorous actions against the Confederacy. Many men owed their lives to Captain Daniel Ellis, of Carter County, who made nearly fifteen trips and guided several thousand men out of East Tennessee via the Cumberland Gap to Camp Dick Robinson, Kentucky. Throughout the war, Ellis served as a pilot in an "escape network" designed to organize recruits and lead them out of East Tennessee. This risky undertaking required great skill since travel took place at night and on rarely traveled paths in order to avoid Confederate patrols. Ellis also served as a reliable communication link between the men and their families. While they were away from their families, Ellis made several trips back and forth across the mountains into Kentucky and later Middle Tennessee delivering letters and packages.[65]

Suffering continued to be widespread for loyal citizens of East Tennessee. Early in 1862, the war was beginning to take its toll on the Confederate manpower. In response, President Davis authorized a military draft. Now groups of irregular Confederate troops known as "home guards" and "conscription officers" roamed throughout East Tennessee ransacking and burning the homes of those who refused to submit to the draft. Unionists became targets for Confederate conscription officers like Colonel Vincent A.

The Dreaded Thirteenth Tennessee Union Cavalry

Left: Captain Daniel Ellis, a native of Carter County who was vital to the Union efforts. He served as a scout and pilot, leading thousands of Union men safely from East Tennessee across the mountains into Kentucky. Later, he was mustered into the Thirteenth Tennessee as a captain. After the war, Ellis published an account of his wartime adventures. He lived in Carter County until his death in 1908. *From Scott and Angel,* History of the Thirteenth Regiment, *facing 144.*

Below: Southern "Volunteers," a lithograph published by Currier & Ives soon after the Confederacy passed its Conscription Law in April 1862. The artist characterized Confederate recruiting officers engaged in what resembles a criminal act. A Confederate has a rope around a reluctant recruit's neck, saying, "Come along you rascal! And fight for our King Cotton." The recruit pleads, "Let me go, I tell you I'm a Union Man, and don't believe in your Southern Confederacy." A second soldier, who prods the man with a bayonet, says, "Blast your Union! Them as won't go in for the war must be made to do it. Go ahead, or we'll hang you on the next tree." *Courtesy of the Library of Congress.*

Witcher, Captain B.H. Duvall, Captain R.C. Bozen and home guards led by William Parker, Bill Waugh and Samuel McQueen, along with many others who made a practice of hunting down and killing Unionists.[66]

As word spread that Ellis was guiding men across the mountains into Kentucky, many loyal men from all over the region traveled to Carter County to meet up with him. This was extremely dangerous, especially for those traveling through the mountain passes between North Carolina and Tennessee. Confederate home guards closely patrolled the region. David Bell, a prominent physician of Carter County, took in a group of fifty men from North Carolina and made inquiries into Ellis piloting them to Kentucky. Because the men had traveled through the night, they were exhausted by the time they stopped at Dr. Bell's home. The following morning, while Dr. Bell was away from the home, his wife, Sarah, and older brother James tended to the men. As Mrs. Bell prepared breakfast for the travelers, Colonel Witcher's Confederate home guardsmen raided the home. Some of Bell's neighbors, who were sympathetic to the Confederacy, had informed Colonel Witcher about the men staying at the doctor's home. The men, who were sitting under some trees, tried to run, but Witcher's men shot them down without mercy. James Bell ran into the yard and tried to stop Witcher, but he fell, wounded from a gunshot. Hearing the commotion, Mrs. Bell ran out to try and save her brother-in-law, but she was knocked unconscious when one of the men struck her. Witcher's men finished off the wounded James Bell by smashing his head with a rock. Before leaving, the men set fire to Bell's home. This group of home guards rode throughout the Limestone Cove area killing other Unionists. Known as the "Limestone Cove Tragedy," Witcher later boasted that he had "rid the world of twenty-one Lincolnites" in one day.[67]

Often, East Tennesseans raised their own companies and then traveled to Kentucky with the hopes of serving in the Union army. One observer noted, "They have sacrafized [sic] their property, left their wifes [sic] & little ones and traveled hundreds of miles in the night (for they dare not travel in day light) to join the United States army, to aid the government of their fathers in puting [sic] down an unholy rebellion."[68] Lafayette Jones and Eli W. Mulican, two Unionists, raised a company of one hundred men from Carter and Johnson Counties with the intention of going through the lines and joining the Union forces in Kentucky. Jones, elected captain of the company, was a resident of Johnson County, Tennessee, while Mulican, elected first lieutenant, had traveled from Davidson County, North Carolina, to join the Union cause. Ellis led the group, but they did not get very far. They made it to Johnson's Depot before encountering Bill Waugh's Confederate home guardsmen. Ellis and Mulican escaped with several of the Union volunteers, but Waugh's men captured Captain Jones. During the struggle, Jones was struck in the head with a gun, inflicting a wound that affected him the rest of his life. Additionally, Jones was robbed of his possessions, including a large sum of gold, and transported to Richmond as a prisoner of war. While it is unclear from the records exactly where Jones was imprisoned or the circumstances surrounding his release, he nevertheless returned to East Tennessee in the spring of 1864, vowing revenge against Waugh.[69]

Lafayette Jones found a willing partner in Daniel Ellis in carrying out his desire for revenge. Ellis had his own reasons for wanting to kill Bill Waugh. Piloting new recruits to Middle Tennessee for the Union cavalry, Ellis returned to East Tennessee loaded with packages and money to be delivered to several of the soldiers' families. Soon after delivering the packages, Ellis learned that home guardsmen led by Samuel McQueen and Bill Waugh had broken into the homes and stolen most of the money. Incensed by the crime, Ellis was "determined to have this money back, or the worth of it." Ellis, accompanied by Jones, who was now a captain with the Eighth Tennessee Union Cavalry, took a company of men through enemy lines into Johnson County with the intention of killing both Waugh and McQueen. The men surprised Waugh at his home, and Jones immediately shot him dead. A search of the home turned up nothing. The group proceeded to McQueen's residence, hoping to kill him as well. However, McQueen was not found at home and no goods or money discovered. Since they could not find the stolen items, Ellis and his men took horses as payment for the money taken from Union families.[70] While McQueen avoided death during this raid, Unionists would take their revenge on him soon.

Not only were individuals attacked for helping conscription-aged men escape to Union lines, but those relatives of Union soldiers who remained in East Tennessee also became targets of violence. William Parker and his band captured, tortured and killed residents from Carter and Johnson Counties. Daniel Ellis accused Parker and his men of burning no fewer than one hundred homes of Unionist families during the summer and fall of 1864. Reportedly, Parker circulated a blacklist or "death list" among his gang that targeted specific Unionist families. John H. Vaught, a sixty-five-year-old resident of Johnson County, was on this list. Vaught's son George joined the Thirteenth Tennessee and was later killed during the war. Parker came to Vaught's house one evening and accused him of aiding other Unionists hiding in the mountains. Parker and his men beat the elderly man, and then Parker personally shot Vaught point-blank in the chest.[71]

Parker and his men also targeted Levi Guy, who had sons serving in the Union army. Parker's men arrived early in the morning as Guy was eating his breakfast. His hands were tied behind his back, and he was marched off to his death. Guy was hanged from a tree about half a mile from his home. Harriet Guy, his young teenage daughter, tried to follow the men in order to help free her father. She was discovered and driven back home by repeated whippings "until the blood ran from her arms and back profusely." Later that evening, Harriet returned along with her mother and younger sister to the place where her father was hanged. She was able to let the body down, and it was taken back and buried. After hearing of their father's death, the sons returned for revenge, only to be murdered by Parker as well. Daniel Ellis, however, pledged "to get rid of this old blood-thirsty tyrant." This would be difficult since Parker, wary of Union bushwhackers, usually surrounded himself with members of his gang for protection. In the fall of 1864, Ellis and ten other men formed a company for the sole purpose of killing Parker. They concealed themselves for days along a regularly traveled route of home guards patiently waiting for Parker. Finally, he appeared, and Ellis recorded that "every gun was immediately let loose" and Parker slumped forward in the saddle. The horse took off, and Parker's body was not discovered until two months afterward.[72]

The strife that ensued between Unionist and secessionist groups intensified in East Tennessee during the course of the war. The violence split families and friendships and polarized the region. Often, an attack made by one side was met with retaliation from the other. This was clearly the case with the Brooks, Tipton and Heatherly families of Carter County. William Brooks, son of prominent farmer Reuben Brooks, enlisted as a lieutenant with the Fifty-ninth Tennessee Confederate Infantry. Young Brooks was a conscription officer and determined to locate Thomas Heatherly's sons, who were in violation of the conscript law. George and Godfrey Heatherly lived about six miles away from the Brooks farm and were among those Union men hiding from Confederate conscription officers. Brooks came upon the Heatherly brothers, who were hiding out near the Stony Creek community. They opened fire on Brooks, and he was killed instantly. News of Brooks's death spread among the Confederate forces in the county, and the Heatherlys became wanted men. Lieutenant Robert Tipton, son of another prominent farmer, Isaac P. Tipton of Carter County, served with the Nineteenth Tennessee Confederate Infantry and was ordered to find the Heatherlys. Tipton reportedly paid a visit to Thomas Heatherly, father to George and Godfrey, and threatened to hang the man if he did not turn in his sons.

The Dreaded Thirteenth Tennessee Union Cavalry

In the meantime, the Heatherlys raised a gang of men and paid a visit to Lieutenant Tipton's home. They tricked him into thinking they were a Confederate company that had been attacked by a Union force at Carter's Depot. The ruse convinced Lieutenant Tipton and his brother Eldridge Tipton, who was a lieutenant with the Thirty-seventh Tennessee Confederate Infantry home on furlough, to go with the group. The men told Robert Tipton they should stay off the main road, as the Union forces were in pursuit. As a result, Tipton took the group to a secluded area. When the group halted, the Tipton brothers realized these men were not Confederate troops and their lives were in danger. Reportedly, it was George Heatherly who placed the gun to Robert Tipton's head and pulled the trigger. Eldridge Tipton was forced to watch the cold-blooded murder of his brother. Instead of killing Eldridge Tipton, the Heatherlys took him farther into the mountains as a hostage. At this time, Captain B.H. Duvall arrived in Elizabethton with a Confederate military force. Duvall had the Heatherlys' young brother, Thomas Jr., arrested for the murder of William Brooks. Duvall threatened to kill the seventeen-year-old young man unless Eldridge Tipton was released. Additionally, Duvall arrested five prominent Union men, including Dr. Abraham Jobe, and threatened their lives as well. Jobe obtained permission to go look for the Heatherlys. This was a dangerous undertaking since many Union men were hiding in the mountains and determined to kill anyone suspected as a conscription officer. Jobe was finally able to locate the Heatherlys and just barely escaped being shot before a member of the group recognized the doctor. After some negotiating, Eldridge Tipton was released. Nevertheless, Captain Duvall had young Thomas killed in retaliation for the deaths of William Brooks and Robert Tipton. Unionists did not dare try to bury the body for fear of retaliation from home guardsmen. If not for the actions of Confederate major Henderson M. Folsom, a native of Elizabethton, the body would have never received a proper burial. Major Folsom happened to be at home on leave when the incident occurred. He went with some other Unionist men to have Thomas Jr.'s body buried. The Heatherlys escaped punishment for killing Lieutenants Books and Tipton, and both eventually enlisted with Union regiments: George Heatherly with the Tenth Tennessee, while Godfrey Heatherly served with the Thirteenth Tennessee.[73]

Throughout 1862 and into 1863, as East Tennesseans continued to endure great hardships, loyalist leaders tirelessly lobbied the Federal government to launch an invasion into the region and authorize the creation of Tennessee military regiments. Horace Maynard met with President Lincoln, and the president was "reluctant still to interfere with his commanding Generals while in the field & before the enemy."[74] Andrew Johnson pressed Secretary Stanton, writing, "The rebel Cavalry are committing the most atrocious outrages upon the people & there are no means to protect them."[75] Once again, Maynard pleaded with President Lincoln in a letter for the liberation of East Tennessee as he invoked the spirit of emancipation. Maynard wrote, "Having provided for the freedom of the slaves, can you not, I beg you, in God's name, do something for the freedom of the white people of East Tennessee?"[76]

In the meantime, Roderick Butler had plans of his own. While the Union army continually stalled on an invasion, he was planning to raise a Tennessee regiment. On his return from the state legislature in 1862, Butler met with John K. Miller, sheriff and one of the most respected men in Carter County. Butler told Miller that he wanted to organize a regiment, take it through the lines to Kentucky and put it in the Federal service. A secret meeting was called, and the men gathered at Elizabeth Smith's house in Roan Mountain. Butler informed those who had gathered that he and Miller were going to raise a regiment of Union men and that Ellis would help to guide men through to Kentucky.[77] Later that year though, suspicion was aroused by plans of a military regiment, and Butler was arrested. He was transported to Knoxville to stand trial for treason, but having no real evidence on which to hold him, Butler was released. Yet the Confederate home guards kept a watchful eye on Butler and his family.

Butler had several sons, none of whom was eligible for the military draft. His eldest son, Richard, was nearly sixteen years old when a Confederate company stationed near the Butler residence enlisted the boy. The officers of the company persuaded Richard to join the army and promised him a horse if he could bring a saddle and bridle. With his father being away on business at the time, the young Butler went with the soldiers. When Roderick Butler arrived at home, his wife told him that Richard had run away and joined the Confederate army. Butler immediately pursued the Confederate company in order to take his son back home. He found the men and his son. Furious with Richard, he made the boy walk home, a total of six miles, with the saddle on his back, whipping him all the way. Once they arrived home, Roderick continued to whip the boy, telling him he would rather see him with "his neck cut from ear to ear rather than for him to join the rebel army."[78] On two other occasions, Roderick Butler was arrested by Confederate officials and charged with treason. Fortunately for Butler, he was released both times due to a lack of witnesses. With the help of friends, he was able to make his way through enemy lines to Kentucky.

The Dreaded Thirteenth Tennessee Union Cavalry

As Union military campaigns finally gained momentum in West and Middle Tennessee, President Lincoln appointed Andrew Johnson military governor of Tennessee. Because East Tennessee was his home, Johnson was particularly sensitive to the suffering of Unionists under Confederate occupation. In his first formal address as military governor, on March 22, 1862, Johnson proclaimed to a capacity crowd in the state House of Representatives, "They may burn our houses, sack our fields, convert our plains into graveyards, and our mountains into sepulchers, but never—no, never, can they eradicate our affection for the Government of our fathers."[79] On the same day of his speech, Johnson appealed to President Lincoln and Secretary Stanton for permission to raise Tennessee regiments in order to strike at Confederate vigilantes. Almost a year after the request, Governor Johnson finally gained consent from Stanton to recruit several regiments of Union infantry and cavalry. This agreement allowed for the formation of the Thirteenth Tennessee Volunteer Cavalry under the command of Elizabethton sheriff Colonel John K. Miller.[80]

Chapter 2

"Rally 'Round the Flag"

The fall of Forts Henry and Donelson to Union forces in February 1862 brought changes to Tennessee. Once these fortifications were under Union control, the Tennessee and Cumberland Rivers were open to Union gunboats. On February 25, Nashville became the first Confederate capital to fall as General Don Carlos Buell traveled up the Cumberland and occupied the city. This began the long journey toward the liberation of East Tennessee. When Nashville fell into Union hands, President Lincoln appointed Andrew Johnson military governor of Tennessee. Along with the duties of governor, Johnson also held the rank of brigadier general, which made it possible for him to supervise the recruitment of troops.[81] As military governor, Johnson inquired from General Buell as well as Secretary of War Stanton "upon whom and to what extent" he should rely for necessary military forces. Stanton replied that the military commanders operating in Tennessee were to aid the governor; however, Buell made a point that these officers operated in separate commands from the governor. Further, Buell added that within "respective limits," the governor should make all military orders through the provost marshal. Any hopes Stanton had of Buell and Johnson working together "effectively and harmoniously" were unrealistic from the very beginning.[82]

In early April 1862, Buell's forces were ordered to assist General Ulysses S. Grant's armies on the Tennessee River. The two-day battle that ensued, known as Shiloh, resulted in Union forces successfully driving Confederate forces across the Tennessee River. Now all of Western and Middle Tennessee were under Union control. Ironically, the most loyal part of the state was still under Confederate control. As soon as Buell's forces moved out, Confederate irregular and guerrilla forces began terrorizing the Nashville area. They burned houses, destroyed barns, tore up railroad track, cut telegraph lines, conscripted men and horses and in general brought misery to loyal citizens.[83]

After Shiloh, Union forces advanced to Corinth, Mississippi, an important Confederate railroad hub. The plan was for Buell and his troops to move eastward into Alabama and back into Middle Tennessee, clearing all remaining Confederate forces. Yet as Buell moved east, he had all available Tennessee regiments join his army in support. Governor Johnson worried about the defense of Nashville, especially with increased Confederate cavalry raids led by Generals Nathan Bedford Forrest and John Hunt Morgan. In particular, Johnson was concerned about the Louisville and Nashville (L&N) Railroad, a vital transportation link allowing the Union army to send supplies and troops to its advancing armies. Johnson communicated his displeasure with General Buell for leaving Nashville unprotected. He sent word to Stanton that Buell had left the city nearly defenseless. Likewise, he complained loudly to Horace Maynard, who was in Washington, D.C., that Buell's withdrawal of troops from Nashville was, in essence, "surrendering the country to the rebels." He continued, "You are well aware of General Buell's course in regard to Tennessee from the beginning to the present moment." It was evident that the irritation Johnson held against Buell dated back to his refusal to invade East Tennessee. Further, Johnson appealed to Lincoln to remove Buell from command on the basis of incompetence. He wrote, "Petty jealousies and contests between generals wholly incompetent to discharge the duties assigned them have contributed more to the defeat and embarrassment of the Government than all other causes combined." In Buell's defense, General Henry Halleck, senior commander of the Western Theater, explained to Stanton that the army needed every available man, as it was about to attack the enemy. In Halleck's opinion, to send troops to "Governor Johnson would be releasing our grasp on the enemy's throat in order to pare his toe-nails." While Lincoln deferred to Halleck's judgment, he later reminded him, "The Governor is a true and a valuable man—indispensable to us in Tennessee."[84]

By the summer of 1862, protection of Nashville still loomed large on Johnson's mind. Confederate raiders continued to harass the loyalist population in the surrounding areas. Morgan's raiders especially held a special place of contempt with Johnson. In May, Morgan attacked the L&N Railroad, destroying freight and passenger cars and a locomotive, and stole between $3,000 and $10,000 from the express agent. Afterward, Morgan sent a telegram to the governor bragging that he had "burned Federal cotton, smashed a train, and torn up a railroad."[85] Johnson reasoned that if the government would comply with his requests, these raids would stop. Learning that Buell needed more cavalry, Johnson telegraphed Lincoln asking permission to begin organizing cavalry units in Tennessee for "home purposes." In response, Stanton officially authorized Johnson "to raise any amount of cavalry in your State that may be required for the service." Lincoln wrote to Johnson in regard to recruitment of troops saying, "If we can get a fair share of them in Tennessee I will value it more highly than a like number most anywhere else,…because they will be at the very place that needs protection." Johnson responded that the troops would be raised, and once "the rebel army can be expelled from East Tennessee there can and will be an expression of public opinion that will surprise you."[86]

While Tennessee cavalry units were formed, Johnson realized that Union commanders were still unwilling to assign units to him for special service. Johnson wanted a military force, a "governor's guard," under his control that could support civil authorities while providing special military capability. Authorization for a guard arrived from the War Department in the spring of 1863, and Johnson moved to transfer the Tenth Tennessee Infantry under command of General Alvan C. Gillem. A West Point graduate, Gillem prior to the war had taken part in the Seminole Wars in Florida. He served as a quartermaster at Shiloh and during the Corinth campaign. From Shiloh, he had written to Johnson asking for the command of a Tennessee regiment.[87]

By the summer of 1863, an invasion of East Tennessee finally became a reality. Major General William Rosecrans, who replaced General Buell, moved his Army of the Cumberland south from Murfreesboro, Tennessee. The Army of the Ohio under command of Major General Ambrose P. Burnside marched from Kentucky into Tennessee through the Cumberland Gap. The Union troops pushed quickly into Knoxville. As the Union army marched into town, on September 2, 1863, they were met by cheering crowds of Unionists.[88] After Burnside arrived in Knoxville, Lincoln indicated a deep concern about recruiting more troops. Enlistment lagged due to continued Confederate home guards; recruiting was still dangerous. Burnside proclaimed to the local population that loyal citizens were encouraged to form themselves into companies. Then, as soon as the companies were organized, they would receive ammunition and equipment."[89]

Roderick Butler began recruiting for the Thirteenth Tennessee Volunteer Cavalry. He distributed the following broadside:

The Dreaded Thirteenth Tennessee Union Cavalry

Rally, East Tennesseans and North Carolinians!
By permission of Major General A.P. Burnside, I am raising a regiment of infantry for the service of the United States, and I appeal to the Union men of the mountains of Tennessee and North Carolina to come forth immediately. Good arms and clothing will be furnished you immediately. Your bounties of money and land will be promptly paid. My headquarters will be fixed in a few days.

R.R. Butler
October 14, 1863

The volunteers gathered at Strawberry Plains, a few miles outside Knoxville, and on October 28 and November 8, 1863, nine companies—A through I—were mustered into the Thirteenth Tennessee Volunteer Cavalry.[90] John Miller was elected colonel, with Roderick Butler serving as lieutenant colonel. Later, three more companies, K, L and M, were added to their ranks. Still not at full strength and needing equipment and training, the regiment moved out from Strawberry Plains on November 23 heading for Camp Nelson, Kentucky, a march of nearly 170 miles. To say the least, it was an extremely difficult march in a "cold, drizzling rain, wading streams, with nothing to eat." Their meager rations consisted of cornmeal and pork, which was used to bake bread on flat rocks or sometimes to fry the dough in grease. While most would not find this very appetizing, the men "ate it with much relish, only regretting they did not have more of it." As they had not received adequate supplies, most of the men were without tents, blankets or sufficient clothing to keep them warm during the cold nights. During one particularly cold night, seventeen-year-old Oliver McClellan of Greene County suffered from the effects of what we now call hypothermia and died.[91] While the men made it safely through the Cumberland Gap, due to Union troops blockading the road through the gap, there was still a real danger of running into Confederate patrols. Private Daniel S. Head of Johnson County was captured during the march to Camp Nelson. At first he was confined in Richmond, Virginia, but when Confederate leaders decided to move prisoners of war away from the Confederate capital, Head was transported to the infamous Andersonville prison camp in Georgia. Like thousands of others, Private Head suffered from appalling conditions, and he ultimately died on April 21, 1864, from dehydration as a result of chronic diarrhea.[92]

After much hardship, the men finally reached Camp Nelson on December 4, 1863. Their spirits were lifted almost as soon as they entered the training camp. The Fourth Tennessee Infantry was at Camp Nelson, and among them were many friends from Carter and Johnson Counties. It seemed the "greatest anxiety" for the men was for their families left behind in East Tennessee, particularly since they were being constantly harassed by Confederate home guards.[93]

The Thirteenth Tennessee, by January 1864, still lacked the number of recruits necessary to bring it to full strength. East Tennessee native George W. Doughty, who was residing in Gordon County, Georgia, when the war began, managed to help enlist a sufficient number of men. He arrived at Camp Nelson with 150 men with the intention of forming a separate Tennessee cavalry unit. However, it was decided to add the men to the Thirteenth Cavalry as Company K in order to finish filling the ranks. These men also were valuable since they had some military experience. Doughty recruited them between July and September 1863; several

Top: Lieutenant Colonel Roderick R. Butler (circa 1863) played a decisive role in the formation of the Thirteenth Tennessee Volunteer Cavalry in 1863. He was commissioned a lieutenant colonel but afterward resigned due to health problems. *Courtesy of Tony Marion.*

Right: Colonel John K. Miller, Carter County, Tennessee sheriff who worked with Roderick R. Butler in the formation of the Thirteenth Tennessee. He was placed in command of the Third Brigade "governor's guards." *Courtesy of Tony Marion.*

The Dreaded Thirteenth Tennessee Union Cavalry

were Confederate conscripts who had recently surrendered to General George W. Morgan at Cumberland Gap. These former Confederate troops hesitated in joining the Union side, fearing they would be shot as deserters if captured. Doughty promised if they enlisted with the Federal army that he would never surrender them, a promise he was able to keep. He reported to General Burnside with a full company of men. Burnside sent him up the Holston River with orders to report on movements of the enemy. Confederate forces under General James Longstreet had laid siege to Knoxville in an attempt to cut off all supplies from reaching Burnside at Fort Sanders. Since Doughty was well acquainted with many people in Knox, Jefferson and Sevier Counties, he was able to acquire supplies for Burnside's army in Knoxville. Doughty and his men loaded boats filled with "flour, bacon, hogs, cattle and all kinds of produce." General Burnside noted that when the siege of Knoxville was lifted, "we had five times as many rations as when it commenced and could have held out a month longer!"[94]

On January 25, 1864, the Thirteenth Tennessee left Camp Nelson as they were ordered to Nashville. The regiment became part of Andrew Johnson's special governor's guard under the command of General Alvan Gillem.[95] Their first order of business was to disperse any guerrilla bands on their march to Nashville. This march was much different than the one to Camp

General Alvan C. Gillem, a Middle Tennessean and West Point graduate who began the war as a captain serving under General George H. Thomas. During the second year of the war, he was appointed colonel of the Tenth Tennessee Infantry. With the rank of brigadier general, Governor Andrew Johnson appointed him commander of the "governor's guard." He accompanied General George Stoneman on his raid into Virginia and North Carolina in 1865. At the end of the war, Gillem was brevetted a major general. *Courtesy of the Library of Congress.*

Nelson. The men were much better equipped with uniforms, blankets and tents; additionally, most were now mounted, giving them a more soldierly appearance. One observer remarked that the "men were all in new blue uniforms with glittering sabers and shining carbines, with rosy cheeks and smiling faces and merry with songs and laughter." One of the most popular songs of the day was the "Battle Cry of Freedom," and as the men marched they sang:

> *Yes we'll rally 'round the flag, boys, we'll rally once again,*
> *Shouting the battle cry of freedom,*
> *We will rally from the hillside, we'll gather from the plain,*
> *Shouting the battle cry of freedom!*
>
> *The Union forever! Hurrah, boys, hurrah!*
> *Down with the traitors, up with the stars;*
> *While we rally 'round the flag, boys, rally once again,*
> *Shouting the battle cry of freedom!*[96]

As new recruits, they were riding high and filled with confidence that, with training, they would be able to take on whatever sort of enemy they might encounter. As they moved closer to Nashville, the first glimpses of war emerged in the form of Union gunboats on the Cumberland River. Frequently on the march to Nashville, scouting parties were ordered out to search for guerrilla raiders. On one occasion, Private Joseph McCloud and Private William Goodwin from Company G were sent out as advance guards. While on patrol, McCloud spied a nearby farmhouse. He left Goodwin and set off toward the house to look for food. Private McCloud was completely taken off guard when an enemy soldier suddenly emerged from the house, making him a prisoner. Goodwin immediately reported the incident to his company commander, Captain Christopher C. Wilcox. Wilcox took a squad of men and went in pursuit. The men successfully tracked down what turned out to be a small group of Confederate guerrillas. Wilcox and his men attacked their camp, secured McCloud's release and took the Confederates prisoner. Later the same day, six more guerrilla soldiers were captured. These patrols continued until the regiment arrived at Camp Gillem, a mile outside Nashville, on February 18, 1864.[97]

Soon after their arrival, several other recruits from East Tennessee joined the camp. They brought many letters and news from home. Since most of these "boys" had never been to a big city like Nashville, Colonel Miller

Sergeant James W. Pearce, of Elizabethton, Tennessee, enlisted when he was just seventeen. Known as Jimmy, he and his fifteen-year-old brother, Columbus, served bravely. After the war, Jimmy studied medicine and attended Vanderbilt University. He practiced medicine in Tate Springs, Tennessee, and died at age eighty in 1927. *From Scott and Angel, History of the Thirteenth Regiment, facing 273.*

found it essential to enforce strict discipline. A camp guard was established, and no one was allowed to enter or leave camp without a pass.[98] Also, the men were introduced to some of their first mounted drills. It was an awkward display at first, with "many amusing, though not serious accidents." After a few weeks of drilling, Daniel Ellis paid a visit to the camp, bringing more recruits and letters from home. The men were "gladdened by letters from dear ones," while many others "received sad tidings from home." George M. Dugger of Company A, in a letter to his brother, shared, "I have some news from East Tennessee…by men just in from Carter Co. Tenn. that the rebs are killing a good many of our citizens and robbing our people of their property and subsistence to such an extent as will reduce our people to starvation if not soon relieved."[99] Ellis remained in camp a few days before making the return trip loaded down with letters and packages for families back in East Tennessee.[100]

Disease was always a problem during the Civil War, and while in Nashville, many of the men contracted smallpox and measles. Dugger reported to his brother, "The health of our Regiment is very delicate at this time. We had the measles amongst us when we came here and since we got here the small pox…cases are sent out nearly everyday to the small pox hospital."[101] He continued that two of his tent mates, Elbert and James Pierce, were very sick. As it turned out, both died just a few days after George's letter. As a result, Colonel Miller, seeking a healthier atmosphere, moved the camp ten miles outside Nashville. Called Camp Catlett, the camp was situated near the Northwestern Railroad line. Here the men could let their horses graze and continue drills and saber exercise. The men were so awkward that some remarked that they "could have handled pitchforks more gracefully and to better advantage."[102]

During the Union occupation of Gallatin, criminals often used the war to mask their activities by taking part in what is termed irregular warfare. On several occasions, detached groups of the Thirteenth Tennessee were sent out after them. One group led by Ellis Harper and known as "Harper's Gang" often targeted the L&N Railroad, derailing trains or stealing supplies. In April, this group attacked one of the trains, capturing railroad laborers. The men were robbed of all their personal belongings, as well as more than $1,000. Many called for the execution of Harper and his gang of criminals.[103] Harper became so notorious that Governor Johnson ordered General Gillem to clear out these guerrillas using any means necessary. Major Doughty was chosen to lead an expedition against Harper. The major took eighty men to try to stop the interference with the trains. While they were unsuccessful in catching Ellis Harper, Doughty's men wounded and captured one member of his gang. He was hanged soon after as an example to the others.[104]

Corporal William Allen, from Elizabethton, Tennessee, who enlisted with Company A. He died from "unknown causes" in the General Hospital at Nashville, Tennessee, on February 28, 1864. *Courtesy of Tony Marion.*

Also at Gallatin, the soldiers encountered a "contraband camp." Before the Emancipation Proclamation went into effect, thousands of escaped slaves made their way through enemy lines and established camps around the Union armies. Contraband camps did not mean freedom, but many slaves believed it was a step toward freedom since the Federal government determined that the Union army would not return any escaped slaves who went through

The Dreaded Thirteenth Tennessee Union Cavalry

Captain Robert H.M. Donnelly was among those dispatched by Major Doughty to help break up a group of Confederate guerrillas known as "Harper's Gang" in Middle Tennessee and Kentucky. Donnelly was later promoted to major. *Courtesy of Tony Marion.*

to Union lines. They referred to the slaves as "contraband" of war. However, many Union soldiers did not feel comfortable fighting a war to free the slaves. This was the case with the Thirteenth Tennessee. In their regimental history, Samuel Scott and Samuel Angel unabashedly declared they "had known the colored man only as a slave and had lost little sleep over him in any way; they were not fighting to free the slave but to restore the Union."[105] Earlier in the war, a group of Northern soldiers had occupied Gallatin and began efforts to educate the slaves. Once the men of the Thirteenth Tennessee arrived, they did not like the attitude of the contraband in the sense that they were equal. They were of the mindset that while slaves may now be free, they were not equals. Many soldiers began carrying walking sticks, and when contraband did not yield the sidewalk, they took the risk of being struck with the stick. It was common for black people to vacate the area altogether when a member of the Thirteenth Tennessee came walking toward them.[106] Alice Williamson, a sixteen-year-old Gallatin resident, commented about the East Tennesseans in her diary. On May 2, she noted that a regiment of "East Tennesseans have come to hold this Post" and continued, "They are the meanest men I ever saw; but they have one good trait they make the negroes 'walk a chalk.'" That night, the school in the contraband camp was burned down.[107]

This type of behavior clearly indicated that the men needed discipline and training. In May 1864, William H. Ingerton arrived in camp to fill the position of lieutenant colonel. Earlier that month, Lieutenant Colonel Butler had resigned his commission. Butler realized he was not a soldier and believed he could accomplish more through his political network. Ingerton was regular army and had formerly served on the staff of General William Sooy Smith as a lieutenant in the Fourth U.S. Cavalry. In 1850, Ingerton, a native of Ohio, enlisted with the U.S. Army. He was just fifteen years old and served with the Second U.S. Infantry as a drummer. He reenlisted twice, and by 1860, he had risen to the rank of sergeant major with the First Dragoons. When the war started, he was serving at Fort Walla Walla in the Washington Territory. Ingerton had an outstanding record as a brilliant soldier.[108] During 1862, he was brevetted twice. The first came after the battle at Shiloh on April 7, 1862, when he was brevetted a captain and then as a major on December 31, 1862, at Murfreesboro, Tennessee. General Smith, in his March 4, 1864 report on the Meridan Campaign, wrote, "Lieutenant W.H. Ingerton, who acted as my assistant adjutant-general, led the charge of the Third Tennessee most brilliantly, and was uniformly distinguished by his skill and dashing bravery."[109] The next month, Captain James McIntyre made his report about the engagement at Franklin, Tennessee, and wrote, "I then ordered Lieutenant [W.H.] Ingerton, with Companies K and B, to charge the battery, which he did in gallant style, capturing the whole battery of six pieces and between 200 and 300 prisoners, killing a captain and second lieutenant, taking…prisoners and following up the charge some distance, putting the enemy to flight."[110] In early April 1864, Ingerton wrote to his wife about the possibility that he would be promoted as a lieutenant colonel for a Tennessee cavalry regiment. His wife, Anna, was residing in Philadelphia, pregnant with their child. The Ingertons had lost an infant son earlier in 1861. He wrote, "I hope God will spare you and the child that you bear for us…I have been raising heaven and Earth to get a position to make us both comfortable and today will crown it with success. The next letter I write I hope to call myself Col. Ingerton."[111]

When William Ingerton was appointed lieutenant colonel, the troops protested. Their greatest complaint was they did not like the idea of being commanded by a regular army man over one of their native officers, particularly since Major George Doughty was in line for the promotion. Talk of violence circulated among the ranks if Ingerton remained in command. In response to this challenge, Ingerton met with the officers, telling them he believed that his experience in the U.S. cavalry could greatly benefit the regiment. He promised to resign after a month if the men were still unhappy. Despite introducing a rigorous drilling schedule and being a stern disciplinarian, it did not take long before Ingerton won the confidence of the officers and the men. He distributed copies of General Philip St. George

Lieutenant Colonel William H. Ingerton, a native of Ohio who began his professional army career in 1850 as a fifteen-year-old drummer for the Second U.S. Infantry stationed in the New Mexico Territory. When the Civil War began, he was a second lieutenant with the Sixteenth U.S. Infantry. He was brevetted a captain at the Battle of Shiloh in 1862 and later that year elevated to brevet major. In the spring of 1864, he took command as lieutenant colonel of the Thirteenth Tennessee Cavalry. He provided valuable training for the regiment. Tragically, he was murdered in late 1864 at Knoxville, Tennessee. *Courtesy of the U.S. Army Heritage and Education Center.*

Cooke's *U.S. Cavalry Tactics* manual to all the field officers and required them to study and make daily recitations. The enlisted men spent much time in drill and saber practice. Every Sunday, the men participated in dress parades and were thoroughly inspected by their officers. Ingerton used a white-glove test on the firearms; if a soldier's gun did not pass, it was returned for cleaning. Likewise, the lieutenant colonel had no patience with men who did not keep themselves and their military equipment clean. At guard mount every morning, the adjutant was instructed to select two men who had passed all their inspections and award a twenty-four-hour pass. Alternately, the two men who were judged sloppy with their uniforms or firearms were assigned the unenviable task of cleaning the horse lines.[112]

By June 1864, there were orders issued that the cavalry be remounted by impressing horses from the citizens of Sumner and surrounding counties. The people, in return, were given vouchers for the value of their horses to be paid by the U.S. government. Dates were set for people to come to Gallatin with the purpose of valuing their horses by the quartermaster and receiving their vouchers. Many citizens made all sorts of excuses as to why they must keep their horses, but Colonel Ingerton generally dismissed them. He told some that they had "brought on all this trouble by their disloyalty." It seemed that Ingerton had a softer heart for those families who contended their horses were the only way to keep their farms going and to keep them from starvation. On occasion, Ingerton used his influence to have those horses returned to their families.[113]

Conscription of horses in the efforts to outfit the regiment did not go over well with many of the citizens. Colonel Miller complained in a letter to Governor Johnson about Dr. George Thompson. Miller, attempting to provide horses for his cavalry brigade, presented Thompson with a voucher for $145 for a horse in his possession. Miller took the horse, but a few weeks later, the animal mysteriously disappeared from the stable. Upon investigation, the horse was found back in the possession of Dr. Thompson, who claimed he had an exemption for this particular horse, keeping Miller from taking it. Miller wrote a letter to the governor venting that Dr. Thompson was "a rebel at heart" and if it were John Hunt Morgan or Nathan Bedford Forrest who wanted the horse "all would be well with him."[114]

General John Hunt Morgan, lithograph. *Courtesy of the Library of Congress.*

There were incidents of soldiers abusing civilians and their property in the surrounding counties. Captain James B. Wyatt of Company M was accused of robbing and destroying the property of Mr. William H. Robinson of Wilson County. Robinson wrote to Governor Johnson, calling himself a "loyal citizen" who had been treated badly by a group of Union cavalrymen. Colonel Ingerton ordered Captain Wyatt to take a detachment of men with three days' rations and proceed south of the Cumberland River to "impress horses to mount the 13th Regt. Tenn. Cavalry." Additionally, Ingerton ordered Wyatt and his men to disperse the men engaged in guerrilla activity for the Confederacy in Wilson County. Robinson charged that Wyatt and his group of drunken men had arrived on his property during his absence and treated Mrs. Robinson very disrespectfully. They entered the house, making a mess with their muddy boots. As they were drunk, some of the men vomited in the house, while others walked with their muddy shoes on the furniture, including Mr. Robinson's own bed. Furthermore, Mr. Robinson claimed the men stole three horses, a saddle, some scissors, a shotgun and $1,300.[115]

Captain Wyatt, after being made aware of the charges against him, wrote to Governor Johnson to explain his side of the story. Wyatt claimed to have arrived on Mr. Robinson's property on June 8, having traced two stolen mules, and found them turned loose in the road. Also, local resident Sanford Casterman informed Captain Wyatt that Mr. Robinson had been "harboring guerrillas." Casterman offered to guide Wyatt to Robinson's place in order to capture the guerrillas. The men arrived and surrounded the house but found no guerrilla raiders there. Instead, according to Captain Wyatt, he did find a horse suitable for the cavalry. Mrs. Robinson told him it was not their horse and did not know how it came to be on the property. Wyatt claimed his suspicions were aroused since the horse had a Rebel officer's saddle. He took both horse and saddle but told Mrs. Robinson he would return the saddle the next morning on his way back to camp. However, the next day on his return, Wyatt reported that neither Mr. nor Mrs. Robinson were at home. He "regarded it very suspicious" and "concluded I would bring the saddle to Camp." Wyatt assured Governor Johnson that the horse and saddle were the only items taken from the property and there was "no man in my Command under the influence of intoxicating liquor." He stated that on the first day at the Robinsons' house he asked Mrs. Robinson for dinner and claimed she at first refused because they were "Yankee soldiers." She did eventually bake some corn bread for them and fried some meat but would not give them a place to sit and eat it.[116] The ultimate resolution to this matter remains unknown; however, Captain Wyatt continued in command of Company M. This would not be the end of controversy for Captain Wyatt though. Later in the war, he had another incident involving civilians that cost him his life.

Despite these breaches in behavior, Colonel Ingerton continued to instill a sense of discipline and military pride in the regiment. On the Fourth of July, the men participated in a dress parade and fired salutes in honor of Independence Day. In the days that followed, drilling and instruction in cavalry tactics resumed. While many men had improved with practice, others were still awkward, for which they received rebukes and lectures from Ingerton.[117]

While the men were away training as soldiers, back home in East Tennessee many of their families faced dire situations. For three years, residents of the upper counties of East Tennessee awaited liberation from bands of irregular Confederate soldiers who continued to harass them. In an effort to gain some relief, petitions were signed and sent to fellow East Tennesseans, such as General Samuel Carter, Roderick Butler and Governor Andrew Johnson. One petition signed by three hundred individuals was sent to General Carter, who was now serving in Knoxville as provost marshal for the East Tennessee region. They appealed to him to use his influence on their behalf. East Tennesseans were especially worried that without able-bodied men in the region, Rebels would harvest the wheat crop and ship it out of the area. Moreover, they warned, unless the people received military assistance, they would be forced to abandon their lands altogether. Therefore, they petitioned for a military force to be assigned to the region in order to drive off guerrilla bands. These residents pleaded with the general to do something for citizens who had "given up all that was near and dear to them on earth, to fight, bleed, and die for the glorious cause of the Union."[118] In response, General Carter forwarded the petition to General William Sherman's headquarters in Nashville, asking for military assistance. At this time, Sherman commanded the Military Division of the Mississippi. At the same time, another petition was sent to Roderick Butler, who since leaving the military had opened a law office in Knoxville. Butler routinely helped his former constituents of upper East Tennessee, and that was why the petition was sent to him. Butler forwarded the petition to Governor Johnson and indicated that since the governor had at his disposal a special guard consisting of three thousand East Tennesseans in the Eighth, Ninth and Thirteenth Cavalry Regiments, they should be used to rid the region of the raiders. The tone of all the petitions was one of desperation, as the petitioners implored, "Whatever is done must be done quickly."[119] At the notion of using the governor's guard for this task, Sherman remarked, "I have always regarded General Gillem's command as a refugee hospital for indolent Tennesseans and…have never reckoned them anything but a political element."[120] However, when Johnson ordered his guard to East Tennessee, Sherman did not interfere.

At the request of Colonel Miller, Johnson traveled to Gallatin and addressed the men before they moved out. On July 19, Johnson delivered a two-hour address, during which time he spoke of the beauty of East Tennessee and explained that he, too, was a refugee from his home. The governor expressed sorrow over the guerrilla war and devastation visited on the people of East Tennessee. He pledged compensation for lost property and promised retribution. Johnson concluded his remarks by telling the men it was time for them to "go up and possess the land."[121]

On August 1, the brigade moved out from Nashville and headed for East Tennessee. While the men had learned much from Colonel Ingerton, they still had not engaged the enemy in battle. The first few encounters with the enemy came as skirmishes with stragglers from the Confederate army near Rogersville, about seventy-five miles northeast of Knoxville. Colonel Miller rode ahead of his men shouting, "There is no better place to die than on the soil of our native country." During the charge, Colonel Miller was slightly wounded. In his report, General Gillem praised Miller, writing that the colonel's "gallant conduct merits your [Governor Johnson's] particular approbation." The general continued that the men of the Thirteenth Tennessee "are improving rapidly and require little more experience to make them excellent soldiers."[122] Soon they would have the chance to gain more experience as they faced one of the most skilled cavalry commanders of the Confederacy.

Chapter 3

"You Have Killed the Best Man in the Southern Confederacy"

Struggling to maintain civil and military authority over the divided state, Governor Johnson wanted to use the governor's guard to rid the state of Confederate guerrillas. In particular, Confederate general John Hunt Morgan was a constant thorn in Johnson's side. On more than one occasion, he had eluded and embarrassed pursuing Union cavalry. Yet Morgan's recklessness caught up to him in the summer of 1863. After launching an ill-fated raid into Indiana and Ohio, he and his men were captured and sent to prison. However, Morgan spent only a few months in captivity before pulling off a remarkable escape in November 1863. After his prison escape, he vowed never again to surrender. Morgan's reputation grew, and his greatness was heralded throughout the Confederacy.[123]

In the summer of 1864, orders from Governor Johnson placed the Thirteenth Tennessee Volunteer Cavalry on a direct collision course with Morgan's Confederate cavalry. The governor's guard was ordered to "kill or drive out all bands of lawless persons who now infest" East Tennessee. Further, Governor Johnson authorized Gillem to cross state boundaries if necessary to achieve this objective.[124] The governor's authorization was directed toward Morgan, who had established a new command at Abingdon in Southwest Virginia. Morgan was appointed the commander of the Department of Western Virginia and East Tennessee, an unenviable position given its confusing jurisdiction and hostile local population. As Gillem's command began its mission, Morgan faced another problem. In August 1864, Confederate officials in Richmond ordered a court of inquiry to investigate allegations of "excesses and irregularities" connected to Morgan's last Kentucky raid. While leading what is known as the "Last Kentucky Raid," Morgan's men plundered stores, destroyed private property and robbed a bank. Confederate secretary of war James A. Seddon relieved Morgan of command pending the outcome of the inquiry.[125]

As Gillem's command rode into Knoxville on August 17, Unionists welcomed them and expected them to expel the remaining Confederate forces—specifically, Morgan's 1,200 cavalrymen and Brigadier General John C. Vaughn's 500 cavalrymen from upper East Tennessee. If this were achieved, the Union armies could access "hay, oats and wheat…abundant in the upper counties, and the corn" the best in twenty years. It would also stop the flow of crops and livestock to Virginia. Finally, they hoped the brigade would destroy the valuable saltworks just across the state border at Saltville, Virginia.[126]

From Knoxville, Gillem and his men marched to Strawberry Plains, the place where many of the men had first mustered into service. Now having returned to the area nearly a year later, the men believed they were well trained and had every confidence in the officers who led them. Colonel Ingerton had trained his men well, and the training would soon pay off. General Gillem sent Ingerton ahead of the main regiment into Rogersville. There, on August 19, Ingerton and the Thirteenth Tennessee surprised the Confederate force. They killed and captured thirty-five Rebels, including Confederate congressman Joseph B. Heiskell. Ingerton returned with the prisoners and a "fine black, blaze-face horse," which he presented to General Gillem.[127]

As the brigade moved back and forth between Bulls Gap, Morristown and Rogersville, the men became frustrated with marching and countermarching. They believed that General Gillem was trying to avoid a fight, but in reality he was caught between Confederate cavalry units of General Joseph Wheeler and General Morgan. Gillem reported that during some of the fighting, Colonel Miller exhibited "almost reckless gallantry" and served as an inspiration to his men. Gillem believed that the brigade was "improving rapidly."[128] Eventually, Gillem pulled back to Bulls Gap to await scouting reports.

Despite being suspended from command and under investigation, Morgan planned a bold move to restore his reputation. He planned a raid into East Tennessee toward Greeneville, a small town with direct access to the vital ET&V Railroad. From there, he intended to capture Bulls Gap, immobilize Gillem's forces and then strike at Knoxville. On the cold and rainy morning of September 3, 1864, Morgan left Abingdon with a force numbering between 1,800 and 2,000 men. The seventy-mile march was

Above: The Dickson-Williams Mansion in Greeneville, Tennessee. This was the home of Dr. Alexander and Mrs. Catharine Dickson Williams. Confederate general John Hunt Morgan was staying at this home in September 1864 when he was surprised and killed by members of the Thirteenth Tennessee. Today, a marker indicates the approximate place where Morgan was fatally shot. *Author's collection.*

Right: Confederate general John H. Morgan and his wife, Mattie. *Courtesy of the Tennessee State Library and Archives, Nashville, TN.*

long, grueling and treacherous. He arrived late in the evening and sent out a detachment of 200 to 300 men to Blue Springs on the Bulls Gap road and then established his headquarters at the home of Mrs. Catherine Williams. Mrs. Williams was the widow of Dr. Alexander Williams and a relative of Morgan's wife, Mattie. A slaveholder and Southern sympathizer, she was one of the wealthiest women in the county. Mrs. Williams had three sons: William, who was a major on Morgan's staff; Thomas, who also served with the Confederate army; and Joseph, who was attached to the Union army. Later, Joseph's wife, Lucy, who was staying at the home when Morgan arrived, was wrongly accused of informing Gillem's troops of Morgan's whereabouts. As he dined that evening, Morgan's plans for military redemption were already going awry.[129]

Just outside Greeneville, Morgan's advance guard captured a teenage boy named Jimmy Leedy.[130] The boy was riding home from the mill on a horse he had up until then managed to hide from both armies. Leedy stumbled into Morgan's men, and they took him and the mare to a nearby farmhouse in search of food. While Morgan's men were eating supper, Leedy escaped. One of the Confederate scouts, Captain James Fry, later wrote they did not pursue Leedy because his recapture was irrelevant to their objectives. Leedy, whose family were Unionists, rode to Gillem's camp at Bulls Gap located several miles outside Greeneville.[131] The picket guard brought the boy to Colonel Miller's quarters, where he reported seeing Confederate troops in Greeneville. Satisfied he was telling the truth, after repeated questioning, Colonel Miller took the boy to General Gillem, where he was again questioned and dismissed.[132]

Seeing an opportunity for a surprise attack, Colonel Miller appealed to General Gillem for an advance on Greeneville. Miller proposed they march to Greeneville, about eighteen miles, that night and be in a position to attack the enemy at daybreak. Gillem strongly disagreed. He argued that a storm was approaching and this would make a night march difficult, if not impossible, to manage. Yet Miller persisted, pointing out that almost every man in Gillem's command was familiar with the roads between Bulls Gap and Greeneville. Gillem agreed after Colonel Miller consented that he would assume full responsibility if the plan turned disastrous.[133]

The Union force at Bulls Gap was divided into two columns. The Thirteenth Tennessee, under the command of Lieutenant Colonel Ingerton, moved out at 10:00 p.m. Two hours later, Gillem and Miller followed with the remainder of the brigade. The march was nothing short of incredible, as it was made during a fierce thunderstorm. Lieutenant Colonel John B.

Brownlow, son of the fiery Unionist "Parson" Brownlow and commander of the Ninth Tennessee Cavalry, wrote, "The night was very dark and the rain fell in sheets; so dark that you could not tell by the sight of the man next to you... The lightening [sic] played along the ground and showed us where to go." Brownlow also revealed Gillem's doubts about the success of the march, stating, "Gillem spoke very discouragingly; he said it was a wild-goose chase; that Miller was responsible for it [he was] really in command of the brigade. I suggested to him that the men might overhear the conversation, and the tone was lowered."[134]

At daybreak on September 4, 1864, Lieutenant Colonel Ingerton and the Thirteenth Tennessee, numbering about five hundred men, took up a position on a ridge just outside

Lieutenant Colonel John B. Brownlow, son of Unionist William "Parson" Brownlow. He commanded the Ninth Tennessee Cavalry and was part of Colonel John K. Miller's Third Brigade. He offered personal thoughts about the death of Confederate general John H. Morgan, as well as criticism of General Alvan C. Gillem's command. *Courtesy of the U.S. Army Heritage and Education Center.*

Greeneville. Ingerton moved his men into position and waited for the remainder of the brigade under Miller and Gillem to attack the town from the front. At that point, an unnamed citizen from town approached Ingerton with a frantic warning: "For God's sake get out of here as quickly as possible, General Morgan is in town with 5,000 men and every one of you will either be killed or captured."[135] Presented with the opportunity to capture a high-profile Confederate officer, Ingerton inquired as to the location of Morgan's headquarters. After the citizen revealed it was at the home of Mrs. Catherine Williams, Ingerton immediately ordered Captain Christopher C. Wilcox to take Companies G and I into town and bring out General Morgan "dead or alive." Meanwhile, Colonel Miller, rapidly advancing from the front, ordered Lieutenant Colonel Brownlow to take his Ninth Tennessee Cavalry along with the remainder of the Thirteenth Tennessee Cavalry and attack from the front. The Confederate soldiers and most everyone in Greeneville were taken by surprise that morning.[136]

Captain Wilcox's men charged down Main and Irish Streets and surprised Morgan's men, sending them fleeing in different directions. Morgan's headquarters at the Williamses' house occupied the block between these two streets. Wilcox sent a detachment to surround the home.[137] Morgan and his top officers were roused by the sound of gunfire. Captain James T. Rogers, a member of General Morgan's staff, later testified that he informed the general the chances of escape appeared hopeless since Union troops had surrounded the house. According to Rogers, Morgan dismissed the notion of surrender, handed him a pistol and asked for his assistance in making an escape. Joined by another member of his staff, the men moved out the back of the house and concealed themselves in some bushes. Rogers recalled that he and Morgan saw a soldier ride up to the fence wearing a brown jacket and they assumed he was a Confederate soldier. However, as they came into view, the soldier pointed his gun at them and demanded they surrender.[138]

The soldier in the brown jacket was Private Andrew Campbell, an Irish immigrant and recent recruit to the Thirteenth Tennessee.[139] When Campbell demanded they surrender, Morgan's companions obeyed by throwing down their weapons, but Morgan, desperate to avoid capture, fled. As he was running away, Campbell fired, and the bullet hit Morgan in the back, passing through his heart and killing him. Witnesses to the shooting said Morgan only uttered, "Oh God!" as he fell to the ground.[140] Because Morgan had been so thoroughly surprised by the Union troops' daybreak advance on the town, he had not put on his socks, coat or vest. Without a uniform, there was no indication of rank; therefore, Private Campbell at the time did not realize that he had killed General Morgan.[141] Captain Henry B. Clay, a member of Morgan's staff, came forward and looked down at the body, saying, "You have killed the best man in the Southern Confederacy." Not until Captain Clay's identification of the body did the men realize it was John Hunt Morgan who had fallen.[142] Campbell later testified that when he saw a man running from Mrs. Williams's home, he ordered him to halt. The man disregarded the command, and Campbell said he fired and the man dropped immediately. He concluded, "I did not know at that time, nor even had the least idea of, who it was I had shot."[143]

Morgan's body was hastily placed on Campbell's horse despite loud protests from Confederates. Captain Wilcox responded that his orders were to bring

Marauding Mountain Men

Lieutenant Andrew Campbell, an Irish immigrant who initially enlisted with the Second Arkansas Confederate Infantry. He deserted and enlisted as a private with the Thirteenth Tennessee in March 1864. He was promoted to lieutenant after firing the shot that killed famed Confederate general John H. Morgan in Greeneville on September 4, 1864. After the war, Campbell moved to St. Louis, Missouri. Records indicate that he died in 1894 and was buried in a pauper's grave. No stone marks the grave. Campbell applied for but never received a pension for his military service. *From Scott and Angel,* History of the Thirteenth Regiment, *facing 384.*

Morgan out "dead or alive" and that was what he intended to do. News about Morgan's death spread quickly through the ranks, and Union troops greeted Campbell with cheers as he rode into camp. Yet as the fight was not over, Colonel Miller ordered Morgan's body to be laid on the ground and covered with a blanket. He then directed Captain Wilcox to assign a guard to the prisoners and the body of Morgan. Miller's men then pursued the Confederates, resulting in a rout of Morgan's troops. At the end of the day, seventy-five Confederates had been killed and over one hundred captured.[144]

It was not until later that evening that General Gillem first learned of Morgan's death. Lieutenant Colonel Brownlow commented to Gillem that this military accomplishment would be enough to confirm Gillem as brigadier general. A surprised Gillem verified the death of Morgan and then telegraphed Governor Johnson with the message, "I surprised, defeated, and killed John Morgan at Greenville [*sic*] this morning." He then assigned a military escort to take the body back to the Williamses' house so it could be returned to the family for burial.[145]

Three days after the death of Morgan, Lieutenant Colonel Ingerton wrote an "Order of Congratulation" commending the Thirteenth Tennessee for "their spirit of gallantry and determination." Additionally, Andrew Campbell was awarded the rank of first sergeant for his role in the routing of Morgan's troops from Greeneville. The next month, Johnson commissioned Campbell as first lieutenant. Brownlow was correct about Gillem's promotion for leading the maneuver that resulted in the death of Morgan. His appointment to brigadier general was confirmed a few days later.[146] Although Gillem had protested the entire raid and learned about Morgan's death many hours after it occurred, he took credit for ordering the march and found no problem accepting the promotions. Yet the accolades were short-lived, as charges of deceit and murder erupted from the Confederates.

News of Morgan's death spread like wildfire. Unionist newspapers such as William Brownlow's *Knoxville Whig* gloated, "John Morgan is no more! And when he died a Thief and Coward expired."[147] Confederate newspapers offered eulogies comparing the character of Morgan to that of a gallant knight. On September 6, the *Richmond Whig* proclaimed, "Another brave, daring and chivalric cavalier has sealed his devotion to his beloved South with his heart's blood."[148] The *Abingdon Virginian* asserted, "The Confederate States have not produced a purer patriot or a more gallant and fearless leader."[149] A few days later, editors for the *Richmond Daily Dispatch* conveyed their regrets and reasoned that the death of such a skilled cavalryman must be the result of an "unfair fight," claiming that "treachery had been used to murder Morgan."[150] Confederate newspapers emphasized the theme of treachery and betrayal. Several sources blamed pro-Union women for Morgan's death. In particular, newspaper articles blamed Mrs. Williams's daughter-in-law Lucy Rumbough Williams as the person who informed Union troops of Morgan's whereabouts.[151]

Because Morgan had been killed not on the battlefield but shot while ungallantly trying to make an escape, accusations of murder emerged. The charge that soldiers of the Thirteenth Tennessee had murdered a defenseless Morgan without warning originated with two Confederate staff officers, neither of whom was present at the time of the general's death. As Union soldiers surrounded the house, Confederate major Charles A. Withers reported that he had urged the general to surrender. According to Withers, Morgan immediately dismissed the idea, saying, "It is useless; they have sworn never to take me a prisoner." Because surrender was not an option, Withers recalled that Morgan recommended they separate to improve the chances of escape. However, Withers stated that as he moved toward the back of the house, he heard Morgan call out to Union troops, "Don't shoot! I surrender." Withers maintained that a Union soldier answered with, "Surrender and be God damned, I know you." At that point, Withers asserted, the soldier raised his rifle and fired.[152] However, this account is unsubstantiated because Withers had already surrendered to Union soldiers inside the Williamses' home before Morgan's attempted escape and eventual death outside the home.[153]

Major William Williams, another member of Morgan's staff and son of Mrs. Catherine Williams, also supported the murder accusation. In his version, Williams claimed Captain Wilcox from the Thirteenth Tennessee Cavalry rode up and took General Morgan's pistols. Then a Union soldier shot an unarmed Morgan at point-blank range. However, Williams could not have witnessed such an exchange since he was hiding from Union captors in the family's smokehouse when Morgan was shot.[154] Despite the lack of evidence, Morgan's top officers, members of his elite battalion and other Southerners latched on to accounts of treachery and murder as a way to explain the untimely death of their hero.

Stories of abuse of Morgan's corpse also circulated. Withers charged that the body of General Morgan was treated with "every conceivable indignity." He claimed that when he was taken to view the corpse it was unrecognizable. The general's body, according to Withers, was naked, except for a pair of drawers, and was thrown in a ditch covered with blood and dirt. Withers recalled that he had complained to Gillem that the Union soldiers were treating the body worse than a dog. To that, Withers said Gillem replied, "Ay, sir, and it shall lie there and rot like a dog."[155] Confederate sympathizers claimed that the body was thrown across Campbell's horse before Morgan drew his last breath. Others alleged that Union soldiers paraded the body through the streets for almost two hours and left it on the train depot platform.[156]

Charges of wrongdoing by the Thirteenth Tennessee Volunteer cavalrymen were so widespread that on September 5, the day after Morgan's death, Gillem ordered a court of inquiry to investigate. Lieutenant Oliver C. French, an aide to General Gillem, questioned Confederate captain James T. Rogers, a member of Morgan's staff and an eyewitness. Rogers testified, "If General Morgan surrendered before he was shot, I do not know it." Additionally, Confederate general John Echols, successor to Morgan as the commander of the District of Southwestern Virginia, launched an investigation to determine if any misconduct or negligence had occurred. Just weeks after the event, both inquires concluded that Morgan's death occurred after he refused to surrender and was not due to murder, betrayal or negligence.[157] This would not be the end of the Morgan controversy, and charges of murder resurfaced in the years following the war.

Chapter 4

"A Night of Horror"

For the remainder of 1864, Colonel John Miller's brigade fought to secure upper East Tennessee. In the days following Morgan's death, the brigade fell back to Bulls Gap, as scouting groups were sent out to keep an eye on the enemy. General Gillem dispatched men from the Thirteenth Tennessee to go through the lines and report on the enemy's position and strength. Reverend Robert B. McCall volunteered to lead this group. McCall had joined the regiment in Nashville in March 1864 in the role of chaplain. Before the war, he had been a citizen of Jonesborough and served the town both as a Methodist minister and a physician. By volunteering, he made himself useful in "looking after the spiritual welfare of the men," and his medical knowledge was also a benefit to the regiment. It was not out of the ordinary for Reverend McCall to volunteer for such a duty; he had volunteered on many previous occasions. As they made their way through the lines, they came upon a farmhouse near Seaton's Mill in Greene County. McCall knew the family to have Union sentiments and believed it was safe to stop and get something to eat. As the men sat down under an apple tree, they were suddenly overtaken by a Confederate home guard patrol. Because McCall had field glasses in his possession, he was accused of spying. The Confederate soldiers took the men to a nearby thicket, robbed them of their possessions and executed them. The records indicate that McCall died instantly by a gunshot to the head. Remarkably, one of the men, Lieutenant Richard H. Allen, survived for a few days after being shot in the head. Allen had removed the bullet from his own head and managed to make it to a nearby farmhouse, where he died a few days later. Robert McCall left behind two young boys, as his wife had died the year before; their grandparents raised the boys. It was said that Robert McCall "endeared himself to the officers and men by his gentlemanly and Christian character."[158]

When a detachment of men led by Colonel Ingerton met up with General John C. Vaughn's Confederate forces about two miles outside camp at Lick Creek, a firefight ensued. Ingerton's men took up a position on a hill facing east that allowed them to see the enemy several hundred yards away. Sergeant Peter L. Barry was sent with a detachment of sharpshooters across the bridge in the direction of the enemy. Barry's men opened fire. It did not take long before they encountered the main force of Vaughn's men. Colonel Ingerton sent orders for Barry to pull back. The enemy formed two lines; one charged across the field under heavy fire from the brigade while the other line charged toward Ingerton's group. Ingerton ordered a countercharge that halted the enemy for a time, but he was forced to pull back when Vaughn's forces began using artillery against them. Vaughn quickly moved to cut off the retreat, and many men who could not keep up were taken prisoner. During this engagement, between twenty-five and thirty men were killed, wounded or captured.[159]

On September 30, the Thirteenth Tennessee once again engaged the enemy near the railroad at Carter's Depot. They made a charge through a cornfield, and the enemy was driven back. Colonels Miller and Ingerton were in the thickest of the fight, with Miller being slightly wounded. The enemy took up a strong position again at Carter's Depot on the west side of the Watauga River reinforced by artillery. While at Carter's Depot, Colonel Miller received permission to allow the men to visit family in nearby Elizabethton for a few hours. For many, this was the first time they had seen their family since joining the fight.[160]

The regiment returned to Bulls Gap in October to find that General Jacob Ammen and his command had returned to Knoxville. This left the Eighth, Ninth and Thirteenth Tennessee Cavalry units along with Patterson's Battery to take care of upper East Tennessee. On the evening of October 27, General Gillem learned that General Vaughn's Confederate force was now near Morristown. The next morning, Gillem moved his artillery up and began to shell the Confederate front line. In the meantime, Colonel Ingerton led the Thirteenth Cavalry on a charge toward the enemy's lines. Both sides were "immediately enveloped." The Eighth Tennessee Cavalry was ordered to attack the left side of the enemy's lines, while Colonel Ingerton regrouped his men and charged the right side of the line. The enemy was completely routed, inflicting several casualties on the Confederate forces, including General Vaughn. In his report to Governor Johnson, General Gillem made special mention of Colonel Ingerton and the Thirteenth Tennessee. He wrote, "Where all behaved with so much gallantry it would seem invidious to mention individuals, but I hope Your Excellency [will] allow me to call your particular attention to Lieutenant-Colonel Ingerton, commanding the Thirteenth Tennessee Cavalry, who led the first charge and broke the enemy's first line without firing a shot."[161] During the battle of Morristown, Corporal Marion J. Garrison, assigned to Company G, was killed in the line of fire. The twenty-year-old corporal called Morristown his home, and after his death, many of his comrades accompanied his body to his home for burial.[162]

Vaughn barely escaped Gillem's cavalrymen; in fact, for a time it was erroneously reported that the Confederate general had been wounded in the fight. It was a crushing defeat for Vaughn as he reported to General Breckinridge, "I regret to say that my command was stampeded at Morristown this morning."[163] Gillem pursued Vaughn back to his former position at Carter's Station on the Watauga River. Believing that Vaughn's forces were on their last legs, Gillem received a report that Confederate reinforcements were on the way. Indeed, the reconnaissance report was true, as Breckinridge, commander of West Virginia and East Tennessee, began to move troops from Wytheville, Virginia, into East Tennessee. Breckinridge assembled a force of cavalry and artillery, approximately 1,800 men, in order to hold East Tennessee.[164]

Gillem, estimating that a much larger force was on the way, wired General Ammen in Knoxville to send him reinforcements immediately. More than likely, Gillem's overestimation of the force facing him came from Confederate prisoners captured by an advance guard. These prisoners confirmed to Gillem that Breckinridge planned to attack at daylight with a large force. Hearing nothing from Ammen, Gillem evacuated that evening to a position at Bulls Gap. For the next two days, the brigade strengthened its defenses. Again he wired Ammen, only fifty miles away, for urgent assistance and at the same time telegraphed "Parson" Brownlow urging him to use whatever influence he might have with the general. General Ammen was not convinced that Breckinridge had superior numbers and confided to Brownlow that it should not be a problem for Gillem's troops to easily "whip them." A short distance from the town on the afternoon of November 11, a detachment of the Thirteenth Tennessee came under heavy fire from the enemy's advance. As the Union cavalry retreated, many were wounded.[165]

At Bulls Gap on the morning of November 12, the battle between Breckinridge and Gillem began. Gillem reported that at 4:00 a.m., the enemy began with an artillery barrage. Confederate forces made several assaults throughout the day in an effort to dislodge Gillem from the gap. The men realized that if the hills were taken then all was lost, and they "fought with desperation," finally pushing the attack back at a cost of over twenty-five dead and wounded. At the same time, General Vaughn attacked the rear on the Knoxville road. The attack was repulsed, and the rest of the day was spent in small skirmishes. The enemy did not renew their assault. Gillem continued to believe reinforcements and supplies were on the way, as all day he "had been anxiously expecting the arrival of a train at Russellville." Yet nothing arrived. Lieutenant Samuel Angel of Company G wrote, "We were now short of ammunition both for artillery and small arms. We had been fighting for four days with scarcely anything to eat and with no feed for our horses. We were surrounded by a superior force who were being daily reinforced and we could hear of no assistance coming to our aid."[166] General Gillem met with his regimental officers and decided there was no other choice but to withdraw since "the forage in the vicinity having been exhausted, the horses were failing fast…the men having fought for four days without bread."[167] The men began the retreat late on the night of November 13, and it lasted until the early morning hours of the next day. General Gillem foolishly withdrew his pickets from Taylor's Gap, two and a half miles below Bulls Gap, which allowed the enemy to pursue without any opposition. General Breckinridge wrote, "The result of this night attack were a good many of the enemy killed and wounded, [and] about 300 prisoners…this force was routed with much confusion."[168]

Gillem reported to Governor Johnson that, regrettably, Confederate forces "charged and broke through our lines, capturing artillery and trains." He also noted losses in manpower, horses and arms and wrote that the men "heretofore fought gallantly" but had become "panic-stricken." The losses of Miller's Third Brigade alone consisted of six pieces of artillery, the entire wagon and pack trains, ambulances and horses, together with small arms and over 150 prisoners. In the retreat, Gillem complained that if reinforcements had arrived when he requested them, the disaster could have been avoided altogether. He also added, "My men were allowed to starve while the storehouses were full and a railroad running to Russellville."[169]

While Gillem blamed the defeat on a lack of resources, it is apparent that personal acrimony among leadership played a primary role in hindering military efforts. The root of this animosity stemmed from General Gillem's constant insistence that the governor's guard reported only to Governor Johnson and was separate from General Ammen's command.[170] This no doubt irritated Ammen, and he took the opportunity to teach Gillem a hard lesson. In his report, Ammen insisted that the enemy did not have superior forces and suggested Gillem had blundered badly. Ammen indicated that he had indeed sent reinforcements but in the confused retreat Gillem's cavalry had literally run over the infantry he sent, causing many of the men to be captured.[171] General Ammen was not the only one who faulted Gillem for the rout. Lieutenant Colonel Brownlow, of the Ninth Tennessee, also placed all the blame for this failure squarely on the shoulders of General Gillem. Brownlow charged that Gillem had reacted too late to the Confederate attack and further claimed the commander was "beastly drunk" during the retreat, riding slumped over on his horse.[172]

As Gillem's forces moved back to a defensive position near Knoxville, Breckinridge followed, creating fear that communication lines may be cut. It is interesting to note that General Ammen now requested assistance, as he reported the enemy's forces to be large, maybe as many as five thousand strong.[173] Breckinridge, however, never made a direct assault since he believed the enemy's position was too strong to overtake. Also during this time, inclement weather hit, streams became "swollen and the roads almost impassable." Yet as Breckinridge withdrew, he believed the attack at Bulls Gap was successful because "the enemy has been driven back nearly 100 miles" and added he did not believe Union forces would "attempt a campaign this winter in upper East Tennessee." No doubt troops who had served under General Morgan, now part of Breckinridge's division, relished the opportunity to avenge their beloved commander.[174]

The Bulls Gap stampede was "certainly a night of horror" for the Union men. A petty squabble between commanders resulted in the death of many men, while numerous others were captured and sent off to prison to die. Brownlow was among those captured by Breckinridge's troops during the stampede. Fortunately for him, the Confederates were not keeping a close watch on the prisoners, and he was able to make his escape "on a Kentucky race horse." Brownlow later wrote he was grateful his captors had not recognized him as the son of "Parson" Brownlow or it could have gone very badly for him.[175] Also, Corporal Isaac A. Shoun of Company D was captured but was able to make his escape by jumping off the train when it arrived at Carter's Depot. Likewise, Captain Samuel Scott, adjutant to Colonel Ingerton, had his horse shot out from under him by Confederate sharpshooters during the retreat. He and many others from the regiment had to make their escape into the woods on foot. They

Captain Samuel W. Scott, an Elizabethton, Tennessee native who enlisted as a private with Company G. He was commissioned a captain before the end of the war. Scott was elected historian of the Thirteenth Tennessee Cavalry Association and worked with fellow comrade Samuel Angel to publish a regimental history in 1903. He died in 1909 and is buried in the Mountain Home National Cemetery. *Courtesy of Jud Scott.*

walked to Morristown hoping to catch up with the regiment, yet when Scott arrived, he saw Confederate troops. Scott sent his sixteen-year-old orderly, John S. Hilton, into town. Because Hilton was so small, the regular regimental uniform pants did not fit; therefore, he was wearing civilian trousers. In this way, he was able to conceal his cavalry jacket and entered Morristown to see if Confederate troops were there. When he reported back, it was as Scott had feared: the enemy troops had occupied Morristown, and they were forced to remain concealed. They finally reached the home of a Union sympathizer who fed them and helped the men get back to their regiment in Strawberry Plains.[176] Nevertheless, countless other men were captured that evening and were not as fortunate to make an escape. They found themselves loaded onto trains and heading for Danville, Virginia, as prisoners of war.

Situated in the tobacco-rich country of Southern Virginia, Danville prior to the war had been a thriving community of nearly six thousand inhabitants. When war broke out, most of its male population joined the Confederate army, and the large tobacco warehouses were converted into supply depots, hospitals and prisons. The first prisoners of war to Danville arrived in the last part of 1863. These prisoners were transferred from Libby Prison in Richmond, which was located 245 miles north of Danville. Confederate general Robert E. Lee had recommended the transfer to Secretary of War James A. Seddon. Lee feared that with Union armies targeting their attacks

Marauding Mountain Men

Officers' prison, Danville, Virginia. *From* War of the Rebellion, *Edisto Album, PR002-347.2; #aa02064. Collection of the New-York Historical Society.*

toward the Confederate capital at Richmond, it would be unwise to keep large numbers of prisoners in the city.[177]

The Danville prison complex consisted of six brick or wooden tobacco warehouses, each three stories high. All the furnishings had been stripped from the buildings, forcing the men to sleep on the wooden floors. The men slept in rows of four, two rows with their heads toward the wall and two rows with their heads to the center. Conditions were insufferable to say the least when the first groups of Union prisoners arrived and only deteriorated further as time passed and more prisoners arrived.[178]

Many men from the Thirteenth Tennessee arrived at the prison in Danville in November and December 1864.[179] Just a few months earlier, the Danville Prison had been officially declared full "to utmost capacity." This meant that over 4,500 men were quartered on the upper floors of the six buildings. In addition to the overcrowded conditions, the winter of 1864–65 was so cold that the Dan River, which ran south of the prison, was frozen solid. Yet prisoners continued to arrive, and the overcrowding meant that some men were reduced to sleeping in tents, enduring extreme cold.[180] The tobacco warehouses hardly offered more comfort or shelter from the cold, as most of the windowpanes were broken out. Many prisoners died from exposure to the cold since their clothes were threadbare and tattered. One prisoner wrote, "There was hardly anything that could be called covering." He estimated that among the men on his floor, numbering approximately 350, "there may have been sixty or seventy scraps of blanket."[181]

Crowded conditions, cold, hunger, vermin and disease all took a toll on the prisoners. Cleanliness was nearly impossible, as one prisoner wrote the fleas and lice "crawled over the ground from body to body" and "in the darkness there was nothing to be done but to suffer with patience." Another prisoner likened the lice and vermin at Danville to the Egyptian plagues recorded in the Bible. Some of the prisoners had requested a gardening hoe in order to scrape the filth from the floors, but the request was denied since such an implement could be used as a weapon. On occasion, men thirty at a time were permitted to go outside the buildings to rinse off with muddy river water, all the while guards prodding them with bayonets. The bathing water was so filthy that one private convinced himself that he was "cleaner by keeping my hands out of its contents."[182]

As the war progressed, food became so scarce and expensive that it was difficult for average Confederate citizens to obtain, to say nothing for prisoners of war. For instance, in Danville by late 1864, the average price for bacon was four dollars a pound, while a dozen eggs would cost five dollars.[183] Prisoners received very little to eat while in confinement, and what they did receive was wholly inadequate. One prisoner described the basic diet as consisting of corn bread and occasionally soup made of refuse bits of bacon. However, the soup was not very appetizing, as the "bacon is rancid and the

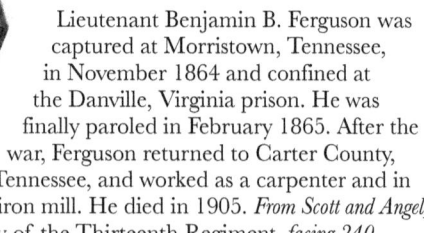

Lieutenant Benjamin B. Ferguson was captured at Morristown, Tennessee, in November 1864 and confined at the Danville, Virginia prison. He was finally paroled in February 1865. After the war, Ferguson returned to Carter County, Tennessee, and worked as a carpenter and in an iron mill. He died in 1905. *From Scott and Angel, History of the Thirteenth Regiment, facing 240.*

vegetables…consisting of stray cabbage leaves and…an article known by us as 'cow pea.'"[184] The soup often contained insects and worms, while the rice was cooked along with rat dung. The water in which everything was cooked was taken from the Dan River, which was very muddy. It accounted for one prisoner to remark that his soup "contained little more than musty rice and spoiled cabbage."[185] Twice a day, under guard, fifteen men were allowed out to the river to obtain one bucket of drinking water for their floor. As men became more emaciated and weak from disease and hunger, they could barely carry the bucket of water.

Because of the filthy living conditions and meager food, disease spread rapidly. Men suffered from chronic diarrhea, typhoid, pneumonia, measles and smallpox. An outbreak of smallpox at the prison sent a wave of fear throughout the community of Danville. A special hospital was established to attempt to quarantine the soldiers with smallpox, but many soldiers died due to the lack of medication or medical knowledge. Wagons could be observed daily carrying the bodies of corpses for burial in a makeshift cemetery.[186] At least fifteen men of the Thirteenth Tennessee were known to have died either during their confinement at Danville or just after being paroled from the prison. One soldier, eighteen-year-old William H. Payne of Company E, was taken prisoner in November 1864 and held at Danville until his parole in February 1865. In response to the news of the parole, his father, Zebulon Payne, also of the Thirteenth Tennessee, wrote a letter to his son. In the letter, the father remarked, "I was glad to here [*sic*] that you was yet alive and out of prison, but was very sorry to here [*sic*] that you was not well."[187] In the letter, the father also expressed hopes that his son would recover his health and be able to join him soon. Sadly, the time spent as a prisoner of war irreparably ruined William Payne's health, and the young man died on April 12, 1865, at a hospital in Louisville, Kentucky.

Ironically, the man who later commanded the District of East Tennessee, which included the Thirteenth Tennessee regiment, had very recently been a prisoner of war. In the summer of 1864, Major General George Stoneman had been attached to the Army of the Ohio as the cavalry corps commander and was serving with General Sherman during the Atlanta Campaign. Stoneman suffered the misfortune of being captured outside Macon, Georgia, making him the highest-ranking Union prisoner of the war. The ultimate irony was that Stoneman was captured while trying to liberate Union prisoners at the notorious Andersonville Prison. He and nearly five hundred of his men were captured by a group of Confederate home guards.[188] After three months, Stoneman was exchanged and in

October 1864 assigned to serve as second in command of the Army of the Ohio under General John M. Schofield.

Colonel William Ingerton was anxious to rebuild the morale of the regiment after the disaster at Bulls Gap. Unfortunately, Ingerton would not survive to accompany Stoneman on his raids into Virginia and North Carolina. As commander of the Thirteenth Tennessee, Ingerton had quickly won the admiration of his men. Still yet, he was a stern disciplinarian and had used tough measures on men who violated military regulations. Throughout his military career, his actions sometimes made him enemies, as in the case of Joshua Houston Walker, a former lieutenant of the Second Tennessee Union Cavalry. Ingerton commanded this cavalry unit in 1863 while serving under General Sooy Smith. During the course of this assignment, Ingerton charged Walker with conduct unbecoming of an officer and gentleman. The charge stemmed from Walker's rowdy behavior at the private home of Mr. and Mrs. James Rafter in Germantown, Tennessee. He had arrived late at night demanding that supper be cooked for him immediately. When Mr. Rafter told him that his wife had gone to bed and no supper could be offered to him, Walker went into a rage. Because he was causing such a commotion, Mrs. Rafter emerged from her room and offered Walker some boiled ham, crackers and coffee, to which he responded by overturning a table, breaking dishes and cursing at them. When the incident was reported to Ingerton, court-martial charges were filed against Walker. The military court in Memphis found him guilty of all charges, and Walker in March 1864 was dismissed from service.[189] Walker reportedly exclaimed he would repay Ingerton for court-martialing him.

Soon after Walker was dismissed from service, Ingerton was promoted to lieutenant colonel of the Thirteenth Tennessee. Walker had obviously kept tabs on Ingerton, waiting for a chance to take his revenge. That opportunity came on the evening of November 25, 1864. Colonel Ingerton and General Gillem had made their headquarters at Franklin House, in Knoxville, and were at this time accompanied by their wives. While waiting for Ingerton to appear at headquarters, Walker had been drinking and was thoroughly drunk by the time he confronted Ingerton. Armed with a pistol, he walked up to where Ingerton was seated. Ingerton, who was holding Gillem's little daughter, looked up, recognized Walker and attempted to push the man away to protect the little girl. After safely handing the little girl back to her mother, Ingerton went toward Walker and attempted to disarm him. In the resulting scuffle, the gun discharged, and the bullet struck Ingerton in the abdomen. A full-blown mêlée erupted as members of Gillem's staff immediately wrestled Walker down, placing him under arrest. Captain David M. Nelson, a member of Gillem's staff and son of well-known Unionist Thomas A.R. Nelson, grabbed a gun and tried to shoot Walker. Seeing Nelson's intention, one of the guards "knocked the muzzle of the gun up" just as Nelson pulled the trigger, and the bullet was fired into the ceiling. Meanwhile, Ingerton was carried to his room, where he suffered in great agony before dying on December 8. Mattie Ingerton, who was now four months pregnant, took her husband's body back to Ohio for burial. The regiment wanted satisfaction for the murder of Ingerton and threatened to gather a lynch mob and hang Walker from the nearest tree. General Gillem, in an effort to defuse the situation, promised Walker would be tried for murder.[190] The death of Colonel Ingerton was a tremendous blow to the Thirteenth Tennessee. Not only had the men lost a great leader but also a role model of military discipline. Given Ingerton's regard for regulation and the customs of service, had he lived, many of the violent acts targeting private citizens may not have happened on Stoneman's last raid.

As it happened, Walker was never tried for Ingerton's murder. Shortly after his arrest, Walker incredibly managed to escape from the jail. The news of the escape greatly distressed the troops in that they wanted Walker to pay for his crime. Yet no one was able to purse him because the regiment was now preparing to move out on an expedition into Southwest Virginia.

In the meantime, Colonel Miller was faced with the monumental task of finding a replacement for Ingerton's position. While Major George Doughty was technically next in line for the promotion, Miller instead chose Captain Brazilliah P. (B.P.) Stacy and promoted him to the rank of lieutenant colonel. This appointment caused a schism within the ranks of the Thirteenth Tennessee. The trouble resulted not so much because the men disliked Stacy but more because one of their own was passed over for promotion. This was the second time that Major Doughty had been denied promotion. The first time occurred when Ingerton arrived to take command. At that time, Doughty did not protest because he believed the regiment would benefit more from having an experienced, career soldier command them. This time, however, Doughty believed he possessed as much experience as anyone in the regiment.

B.P. Stacy was a native of Pennsylvania and had relocated to Ripley, Ohio, before the war, where he worked as a teacher. According to the 1860 census, Stacy boarded with the Joseph Chase family, along the Kentucky and Ohio border, very close to the region known for its work on the Underground Railroad.[191] When the war began, Stacy volunteered with the Seventh Ohio Cavalry and was quickly appointed sergeant major of the regiment. Stacy's

Lieutenant Colonel Brazilliah P. (B.P.) Stacy, a schoolteacher from Ripley, Ohio, who initially volunteered with the Seventh Ohio Cavalry. He came to Knoxville, Tennessee, as part of General Burnside's occupation force and was placed on Colonel Miller's staff. After William Ingerton's death, Stacy was commissioned lieutenant colonel of the Thirteenth Tennessee. After the war, he and Samuel Angel went into business together in Knoxville. He died there in 1882. *Courtesy of Tony Marion.*

regiment pursued General John H. Morgan through Kentucky, Indiana and Ohio before finally capturing him. Then when Burnside's army marched into East Tennessee, the Seventh Ohio was part of the liberation force. General Samuel P. Carter recommended Stacy to Colonel Miller in September 1863 because he believed Stacy could add some much-needed military experience to the regiment.[192]

As a result of his decision to promote Stacy over Doughty, Colonel Miller met heated resistance. Doughty and his friends protested, while Miller reasoned that Stacy was better suited to the position with his "greater experience and longer service in the army." Doughty refused to accept the decision, so Miller had him arrested for insubordination. Eventually, Gillem defused the situation by appointing Doughty as his chief of staff.[193]

Chapter 5

STONEMAN'S "COSSACKS"

Following the chaotic rout at Bulls Gap on November 13, 1864, Gillem's troops limped back to Knoxville. The men needed time to recuperate from the beating they had suffered at the hands of Breckinridge's force. Morale was low, and upper East Tennessee remained under Confederate control. The soldiers feared for their families still under enemy oppression. The situation was so desperate that some officers resigned their commissions in order to return home and assist their loved ones. John L. Hyder, second lieutenant of Company C, resigned explaining that his family in Carter County was on the verge of starvation. He wrote, "I regard it my duty above all others to protect and comfort my suffering family."[194]

During this time, General George Stoneman began refitting and reorganizing his command in preparation for a raid into Southwest Virginia. In his communication to General John Schofield, commander of the Army of Ohio, he proposed the details of his raid with the aim of not only bolstering the morale of his command but also redeeming his reputation. Stoneman's objectives included pushing the Confederate forces out of upper East Tennessee, destroying the important Virginia & Tennessee (V&T) Railroad line from Bristol to Wytheville and rendering the vital saltworks and lead mines in Southwest Virginia useless. Although the Federal government realized the importance of the railroad, saltworks and lead mines to the Confederate war machine, surprisingly, they all remained operational until late in 1864. Stoneman wanted to change this.[195] The Thirteenth Tennessee now became an important part of Stoneman's

THE DREADED THIRTEENTH TENNESSEE UNION CAVALRY

Major General George Stoneman led Union troops during the last months of the war into Southwest Virginia and Western North Carolina. The Thirteenth Tennessee accompanied him on the last raid, and he referred to them as "Cossacks." *Courtesy of the Library of Congress.*

raid into Southwest Virginia. They were eager to liberate their homes still behind enemy lines in East Tennessee.

Stoneman proposed another objective to General Schofield: cross into Western North Carolina and free Union prisoners of war at the Salisbury Prison camp. Stoneman wrote to Schofield, "I hope you will not disapprove…I owe the Southern Confederacy a debt I am very anxious to liquidate." Schofield replied that he was in favor of pushing the enemy back into Virginia and destroying the railroad and saltworks. However, he asked Stoneman to wait on the second part of the plan for now.[196]

While General Schofield was willing to give Stoneman a chance to redeem his reputation, General Grant, commander of the Union armies, had no confidence in Stoneman. He wrote of Stoneman to Secretary of War Edwin Stanton, "I think him one of the worthless in the service and who has failed in everything instructed to him." In fact, unbeknownst to Stoneman at this time, General Grant wanted Schofield to remove Stoneman from command. Schofield received Grant's communication a day before giving Stoneman the go-ahead for his Virginia raid. While Grant did not have any confidence in Stoneman, writing, "I am not in favor of using officers who have signally failed when instructed with commands in important places," he conceded that he was content to leave it up to General Schofield's discretion, and the order was rescinded.[197]

Stoneman's raid pitted the Thirteenth Tennessee once again against its longtime adversaries under the command of Generals Vaughn and Breckinridge. It also marked the first action since the humiliating defeat at Bulls Gap. The men of the Thirteenth Tennessee, just like Stoneman, were anxious to engage the enemy and restore their reputation. The regiment left Knoxville on December 10, moving in the direction of Bean's Station, where it joined up with Major General Stephen Burbridge's command from Kentucky. Burbridge and his men had suffered a demoralizing defeat at Saltville, Virginia, earlier in the year and were eager for a second chance at victory. So it appeared everyone had scores to settle on this raid.[198]

That evening, a supply train arrived from Knoxville, and the men received a week's rations along with all the ammunition they could carry. Just as they moved out from Bean's Station headed toward Rogersville, a steady, soaking rain began to fall. That evening, they were able to take shelter and somewhat dry their clothes, as they had been completely soaked through. Before reaching Rogersville, the regiment encountered the enemy. Lieutenant Colonel Stacy ordered Captain Wilcox to take Company G and charge across the bridge. As he did, the enemy was pushed back. No more fighting took place until the regiment reached Kingsport on December 13. The enemy had taken a position on the bluff of the Holston River. This was General John Morgan's old command, and Colonel Richard Morgan, brother to John, led the men. Gillem's forces were ordered to charge across the Holston River and up the bluff. The charge was made under heavy fire. Colonel Morgan was captured along with nearly two hundred other Confederate soldiers. Additionally, an entire wagon train of supplies was captured.[199]

General Burbridge and his troops rode ahead into Bristol and engaged the enemy. The Thirteenth Tennessee was dispatched to reinforce Burbridge's division. At Bristol, the combined force captured a significant part of Vaughn's brigade thanks to some innovative thinking by Stoneman. The Union force captured a Confederate telegraph operator in Bristol. General Stoneman forced the operator to send a dispatch to Vaughn indicating that the road was clear and to send troops to Abingdon. Stoneman threatened to hang the operator if he warned Vaughn of the true situation. Stoneman then ordered part of his force west to destroy the railroad tracks after the train containing Vaughn's troops had passed. Tracks were also destroyed east of Bristol, trapping the train. When the train pulled into the depot, Burbridge's troops, supported by the Thirteenth

THE DREADED THIRTEENTH TENNESSEE UNION CAVALRY

Captain James B. Wyatt, a native of Abingdon, Virginia, initially volunteered with the Fourth Tennessee Infantry. He joined the Thirteenth Tennessee in February 1864 while it was in Nashville, Tennessee. He was killed in his hometown of Abingdon, Virginia, after intentionally setting fire to some Confederate sympathizers' homes in town. *From Scott and Angel, History of the Thirteenth Regiment, facing 369.*

Tennessee, were waiting. Over five hundred Confederate troops were captured and the train destroyed. Burbridge's force advanced toward Abingdon while the Thirteenth stayed behind and destroyed any remaining Confederate supplies at Bristol.[200]

The regiment proceeded to Abingdon, and as it passed through the town, Captain James Wyatt of Company M asked permission to remain there a short time since this was his hometown. Major Joseph Wagner refused the request because he knew Wyatt had ulterior motives for wanting to stay. Apparently, Wyatt wanted to take revenge against some of the citizens in town who had mistreated him for siding with the Union early in the war. Wyatt disobeyed orders and proceeded to set fire to several buildings in town. Several citizens witnessed the action, and as Wyatt was leaving, they pursued him on their horses. During the chase, Wyatt's horse fell, allowing the men to catch up to him. He was shot and killed by the townsmen.[201]

Learning that General Vaughn was moving east on a parallel road north of the brigade, the Thirteenth led an advance toward Glade Spring, Virginia. The goal was to intercept Vaughn before he could reach Marion, nearly twenty miles away. Sharpshooters and an advance guard led by Lieutenant Peter L. Barry engaged General Vaughn just outside Marion. The regiment charged into town at daybreak. In the near darkness, the men became confused and fired on one another. Captain William Gourley, one of the original bridge burners, was killed during the attack. He saw a Confederate officer near him and struck him with his sword. However, the enemy officer fired, and Gourley fell dead.[202]

After Vaughn's troops were finally driven out of Marion, some men of the Thirteenth Tennessee, enraged at Captain Gourley's death, set fire to the house where he had died. From Marion, there was a continuous battle for several miles as the regiment moved toward Wytheville. The enemy made a stand and launched an artillery barrage on Gillem's cavalry. General Gillem ordered Captain Patrick Dyer to charge the enemy artillery. Dyer captured an artillery piece, and the regiment followed. They dispersed Vaughn's force and captured nearly two hundred prisoners, four pieces of artillery and the supply wagons. Ironically, the artillery captured were pieces the regiment had lost at Bulls Gap.[203]

Captain William M. Gourley, a native of Carter County who very early in the war actively supported the Union cause. He participated in the burning of the Holston River Bridge and later went through enemy lines with Daniel Ellis to join the Fourth Tennessee Infantry. Once the Thirteen Tennessee Cavalry was formed, Gourley transferred to the regiment. He was killed in action on December 16, 1864, in Marion, Virginia. *From Scott and Angel,* History of the Thirteenth Regiment, *facing 128.*

At Wytheville, the regiment destroyed a large cache of ammunition stored at a local church. Captain Scott recalled, "When the flames reached the ammunition, the exploding cartridges of bursting shells and the lurid flames of the burning building presented a grand spectacular scene never to be forgotten by those who witnessed it." General Stoneman ordered another part of his command to destroy the lead mines and burn the railroad bridge across Reedy Creek. The Union raiders met little resistance as they approached the lead mines. There was only a small Confederate force assigned to the mines, and it retreated at the sight of Stoneman's men. The only major obstacle for the Union force was crossing the frigid New River in order to get to the mine. Crossing successfully, they disabled the mine within two hours. The mine offices, storehouses, stables, crushing machine, bellows, furnaces and even the sawmill and gristmill were destroyed.[204]

The lead mines in Wythe County were well established when the war began. The ore was smelted on site and sent ten miles north to Max Meadows. Then the lead was loaded onto the V&T Railroad and transported to Richmond, Knoxville and Chattanooga where ammunition was manufactured. Lead shot was also produced locally in Wythe County. It is estimated that nearly 3.5 million pounds of lead were produced in Wythe County during the war, which constituted about one-third of the lead consumed by the Confederacy.[205]

The regiment crossed Walker's Mountain in preparation of an attack on Saltville. Their objective: destroy the saltworks. Amid a downpour, soldiers could hear nearby fighting between the forces of Burbridge and Breckinridge. Before reaching the top of the mountain, the regiment was ordered back. Several men feared that General Stoneman was about to surrender the entire command. Many of the regiment's officers and men had been formally conscripted by the Confederacy and then deserted to join the Union army. They feared that, if captured, they would be executed. So they left the army and hid in the mountains. Later, many returned to their units.[206]

However, Stoneman did not surrender. Instead, he ordered the Thirteenth Tennessee to make camp near Seven Mile Ford, a few miles from King's Salt Works at Saltville. Meanwhile, Confederate forces had established a redoubt called Fort Breckinridge. The Thirteenth Tennessee in conjunction with Gillem's division broke camp and fought to within 1,500 yards of the fort. General Burbridge's command on the right was instructed to attack simultaneously with General Gillem's forces. As darkness fell, General Stoneman arrived on the scene and ordered Lieutenant Colonel Stacy to take his command and "dash into town, commence burning, shooting" and generally cause "as much confusion as possible."[207] Lieutenant Colonel Stacy and the Thirteenth Tennessee successfully carried out their orders. As part of the men burned the town, the rest charged up the hill toward Fort Breckinridge. Hearing the commotion and seeing the town on fire, Generals Burbridge and Gillem began their assault. Meanwhile, Stacy's men were successful in capturing guns and taking prisoners (two of whom were commissioned officers). Stacy's only losses were two horses.[208] The next morning, Stoneman's men destroyed the saltworks. Stoneman personally recognized Lieutenant Colonel Stacy and the men of the Thirteenth Tennessee in his official report, writing, "Colonel Stacy and the Thirteenth Tennessee Cavalry is due the credit of having acted the most conspicuous part."[209]

His objective accomplished, Stoneman withdrew his forces and moved into camp during a heavy snowstorm. Without protection of tents or any shelter, they suffered greatly from the bitter cold. The night spent in and around Fort Breckinridge was dreadfully cold, and no fires were allowed except inside the fort itself. The next day, the regiment began the march back to Tennessee. It was so cold that the men had to constantly keep their feet moving or else their boots would freeze in the stirrups. Nevertheless, Stoneman, in his report, recorded, "The conduct of the command I cannot speak in terms of too high praise," continuing that despite "long marches, sleepless nights, hunger or hardships," no one complained.[210] The entire raid into Southwest Virginia had taken approximately twenty days, during which time Stoneman's command marched a total of 870 miles, or more than 40 miles a day. Despite the hardship, morale significantly improved throughout the Thirteenth Tennessee. They believed they had avenged their defeat at Bulls Gap. Moreover, the raid liberated upper East Tennessee. Confederate forces had been dispersed, and

Captain Thomas J. Barry enlisted with Company E in 1863 as first lieutenant and was later promoted to the rank of captain. He participated in the December 1864 attack on Saltville, Virginia. After the war, he returned to his home in Johnson County and was a schoolteacher and ran a flour mill until his death in 1909. *Courtesy of Tony Marion.*

they felt their families were now safe. As they moved into winter quarters at Knoxville, they were satisfied to know that East Tennessee was firmly under the control of Union forces and they had played an important part.[211] Also with the success of the raid, General Schofield congratulated Stoneman, writing that the raid had vindicated his "reputation as a general." He added the information about how General Grant wanted him relieved of command but that he worked to have the order rescinded. He shared this information with Stoneman because while Schofield was pleased with the outcome of the raid, he was disappointed in Stoneman's failure to make regular reports. He wanted Stoneman to know that he had supported him and that he expected better communications in the future. Although the raid into Southwest Virginia destroyed vital parts of Confederate salt and lead production facilities, surprisingly, before the end of the war, both salt and lead works were once more operational. This meant that in the spring of 1865, Stoneman would visit the area again.[212]

In February 1865, General Grant was ready for Stoneman to carry out the second part of the plan outlined the previous November. General Grant explained to Stoneman that the purpose of his raid into North Carolina was "to destroy [and] not to fight battles."[213] In turn, Stoneman wrote to General Gillem, "I have just received orders from General Grant directing a movement, in which your fine body of Cossacks is to play a very important part, and I would advise you to put them in condition to take the field as soon as possible."[214] Stoneman's use of "Cossack," denoting Slavic cavalrymen known for ruthless warfare, was a proper description since East Tennessee and North Carolina soldiers under Stoneman's command pillaged, burned and looted during the march into Western North Carolina. As Stoneman's raiders passed through various towns and counties, property of Southern sympathizers was routinely destroyed.[215] In many ways, Stoneman's "Cossacks" were similar to Sherman's "bummers" who destroyed anything the Confederacy could conceivably use in the war effort.[216]

The Cavalry Division, now designated under the District of East Tennessee, was under command of Brigadier General Gillem. There were three brigades that constituted this division. The First Brigade, commanded by Colonel William J. Palmer, consisted of the Fifteenth Pennsylvania, the Twelfth Ohio and the Tenth Michigan Cavalry Regiments. The Second Brigade, commanded by Brevet Brigadier General Simeon B. Brown, was made up of the Eleventh Michigan and the Eleventh and Twelfth Kentucky. Finally, Colonel John Miller was assigned to lead the Third Brigade, made up of the Eighth, Ninth and Thirteenth Tennessee Cavalry units.[217]

Marauding Mountain Men

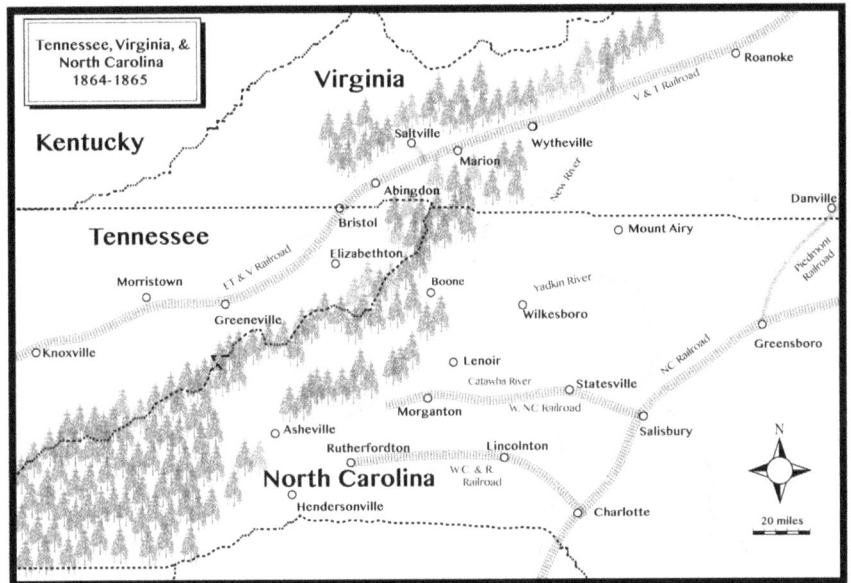

Map showing the areas of Tennessee, Virginia and North Carolina in which the Thirteenth Tennessee was involved during the last months of the war. *Author's collection.*

On March 23, Gillem's Cavalry Division headed out and marched through Morristown, where they were met with a "cordial, hearty welcome from the loyal citizens." They were given a grand sendoff as "people came from all the surrounding country to see us and while perched on their rail fences greeted us with smiles."[218] Marching over the mountains into North Carolina proved to be a dangerous undertaking, particularly along some of the mountain passes. As they traveled along one of the mountain passes near the top of Stone Mountain, the path was so close to the edge of the cliff that some horses and mules fell into the dark ravine below. The march at times was made in darkness, and that made it all the more difficult to follow the path. It was made easier when some residents "built fires along the road at dangerous places and also at difficult fords over the mountain streams."[219]

It was a homecoming for some of the men in the Thirteenth Tennessee as the regiment marched through portions of Western North Carolina. Many had abandoned their homes to avoid Confederate conscription and made their way across the state line into Tennessee. This was true for Sergeant James C.J. Lewis of Watauga County and Private Andrew Greer of Ashe County. The eighteen-year-old Lewis avoided Confederate home guards and slipped through the mountain pass to muster into service with the Thirteenth

Tennessee. Greer left his family farm and crossed the state line to join the regiment. His brother Joel, who had deserted from the Confederate army, later joined him. As they marched back through their old homeplaces, it was bittersweet for Andrew Greer since Joel had been killed during the retreat from Bulls Gap.[220] Indeed, throughout the war there was another virtual civil war that took place in the mountains between the neighboring communities. As a result, the North Carolina and East Tennessee "Cossacks" exacted their version of justice, leaving a path of destruction in their wake.

In some communities such as Banner Elk, pro-Union families were spared hardship since they remained on good terms with both the Union and Confederate sides. For instance, the Union army respected them since they fed and provided shoes for those soldiers escaping from Salisbury Prison. Sometimes they even served as guides, taking the prisoners across the mountains into East Tennessee. Likewise, the Confederate home guard spared them because many of the men worked at the nearby forge making wrought iron for the Confederacy.[221]

Nevertheless, the community of Boone was not spared. Its residents were taken off guard with the arrival of Stoneman's raiders. After the town surrendered, Stoneman recorded it was the "first indication the people have had of our movements."[222] The jail was burned by order of General Gillem, and in doing so, all the Watauga County records were destroyed. While this brought about a firm reprimand from General Stoneman, the destruction would continue as Gillem and the dreaded Thirteenth Tennessee would do little to endear themselves to the residents of North Carolina. Near Boone, along the Wilkesboro Road was a cotton mill owned by Rufus Patterson, known as Patterson's factory located on the Yadkin River. This area of the Yadkin Valley was very fertile, supplying Colonel Miller and his men with ample corn and bacon. Miller's orders were to supply his command, destroy any excess and then burn the factory. Again, General Stoneman regretted this action taken by Gillem because of the importance of the mill not only to the local residents but also to East Tennessee. Gillem ordered the mill burned because, in his opinion, the Union "government had been too lenient, and rebels must look out for consequences."[223]

The division continued to follow the Yadkin River, but at this point the march became extremely difficult as the regiment endured several days of constant, driving rain. Colonel Palmer's First Brigade with considerable difficulty made it across the river; however, several men drowned in the process. By the time Miller's Third Brigade arrived, the water had risen significantly higher, thus making it impossible to cross. When Stoneman arrived, he was angry that part of his command was on one side of the river while the other part was now unable to cross. His orders for the lead brigade were to not get too far ahead of the others, and now the rain slowed their advance. Stoneman swore under his breath and grumbled, "Palmer on one side of the river with those Pennsylvanian boys and me on this side! Gillem, I am going to see what you have." What occurred next would not improve his mood at all. Apparently, many in Gillem's command had stumbled upon several whiskey stills and were in no condition to stand formation. As one Pennsylvania soldier noted, "With the rain coming down in torrents and mud knee-deep, and the stuff warm in the still, our brave allies were driven to drink." Worse yet, they had climbed into carriages that had been confiscated along the way, forming what resembled a mile-long caravan. For Stoneman, it was an infuriating spectacle of drunkenness, with carriages filled with the East Tennessee soldiers passing before him, "their big boots sticking out in all directions." Stoneman held the officers responsible and would occasionally stop "the parade and make a general reduction of captains and lieutenants."[224] As night began to fall, Stoneman made camp. The next morning, the rain had ceased, and after a good night's sleep the "wounded" were in a better condition to continue the march. The men marched through Jonesville and Dodson, making camp at Mount Airy.

The circumstances of the war were changing quickly, and Stoneman soon found his command in the middle of converging Confederate forces. On April 2, as Stoneman's men made camp at Mount Airy, Confederate general Robert E. Lee ordered Richmond and Petersburg to be evacuated. It appeared that Lee would begin retreating to the southwest in order to join forces with other Confederate troops. Specifically, in Southwest Virginia, General John Echols still had under his command between four and five thousand infantry and four brigades of cavalry. Echols concentrated his forces at Christiansburg, Virginia, and waited for Lee. In order to hit multiple targets, Stoneman divided his forces into detachments with special assignments. These groups played a decisive role in Lee's surrender. Colonel Miller chose five hundred men from his Third Brigade and raided Wytheville. Stoneman ordered the detachment to march on the town and destroy supplies at the depot along with the railroad bridges over Reedy Creek and at Max Meadows. As Miller's detachment reached the New River, they found it too swollen to cross due to heavy rain. They found a citizen who lived near the river to pilot a few of the men across. Once across, they built a fire to indicate which place to ford the river. Lieutenant Colonel Stacy took the first group across safely, but some of the men who followed on smaller mounts struggled to cross. Private William

Jenkins at this time was riding a mule and seriously considered remaining behind. Nevertheless, as all the others had made it across safely, Jenkins decided to try and cross on the mule. It was a bad mistake. Jenkins would have surely drowned if Colonel Miller had not rescued him. After crossing the river, the men reached Wytheville the following day, having traveled fifty-five miles on virtually nothing to eat.[225]

At Wytheville, Miller's command destroyed bridges and a depot of supplies that amounted to a large quantity of ammunition and nearly ten thousand pounds of powder. As they were busy destroying supplies, Miller's troops were caught off guard when Confederate colonel Henry L. Giltner's cavalry brigade attacked. After a daylong skirmish, Miller broke off the attack, suffering a loss of thirty-five killed, wounded and missing. Private Jenkins, who earlier had nearly drowned, was among those captured by the enemy. Despite his losses, Miller had scored a strategic victory, and the detachment moved back across the river at Porter's Ford. Giltner's cavalry did not pursue, and after a brief rest, Miller's men destroyed the lead mines that had been repaired from Stoneman's earlier raid. Miller reported his activities to Gillem, who in turn ordered the group to move through Hillsville to Taylorsville, Virginia. During the night, a few soldiers left camp on a foraging expedition and returned later carrying two barrels of brandy. To avoid a repeat of the disgraceful Yadkin River episode, Lieutenant Colonel Stacy ordered "the heads knocked out of the barrels and the contents emptied."[226] At Taylorsville, Miller's force rejoined Stoneman's division and returned to North Carolina.

On April 9, Stoneman's troops were concentrated at Danbury, North Carolina, and moving toward Germantown. By this time, there were several hundred former slaves who were following along behind. Because his plans required quick movement, Stoneman worried the contraband would hinder military operations, so he sent a detachment to transport them to East Tennessee. Meanwhile, the cavalry division was ordered to burn textile mills that manufactured military clothing for the Confederacy. Also, the North Carolina Central Railroad to Greensboro and the Danville & Greensboro Railroad were destroyed as the raiders moved toward Salisbury.[227]

Stoneman targeted the town of Salisbury because it had an important railroad junction and was the location of a notorious Confederate prison. On April 12, his forces moved to within two miles of the town. As they approached Grant's Creek bridge, the planks had all been removed by the Confederate troops under the command of General William M. Gardner. Gardner had between five and eight hundred soldiers and artillery. According to reports, Gardner's forces consisted of "galvanized Irish" (former prisoners of war who enlisted with the Confederate army in exchange for freedom), government employees, volunteer citizens and home guardsmen, men who possessed little, if any, combat experience.[228]

Gillem deployed his artillery and concentrated his division at the bridge. Major Donnelly of the Thirteenth Tennessee was ordered to take about one hundred men and cross the creek in cooperation with other detachments and engage the enemy. As soon as the enemy was engaged, the Thirteenth under Lieutenant Colonel Stacy dismounted and moved forward on foot. The Eighth and Thirteenth Tennessee had replaced the flooring on the bridge. The men charged across the bridge under heavy fire, and the enemy was quickly dispersed. Stacy's charge was met with little resistance, and many of Gardner's troops intentionally fired over their heads. Many "galvanized Irish" cheered at the sight of the American flag and surrendered to Stoneman almost as quickly as the firing started. In fact, the fighting, which began at daylight, was virtually over by eight o'clock that morning. The Confederate retreat soon became a rout as they scattered throughout the town and into the surrounding woods.[229]

As the Union troops rode into the town of Salisbury, residents held their breath, unsure of what might happen next. "Cossacks" seemed to appear from all directions and rode into the town's square,

Major Robert H.M. Donnelly, a carpenter from Johnson County, Tennessee, who among other loyalists left his home to enlist with the Union army. In December 1864, he led a successful charge against Fort Breckenridge in the Battle of Saltville, Virginia. After the war, he served as a postmaster and owned a mercantile store in Rheatown, Green County, Tennessee. *Courtesy of Tony Marion.*

where the mayor met them under a flag of truce. Reportedly, one soldier with blood running down his face let out a loud yell, and the flag was cut down. Others stopped to let their horses feed on the corn, which was "poured out on the pavements of every street in town." Mrs. Mary Ellis of Salisbury and her four daughters tried to carry on with their daily activities despite the battle being fought around them. They had just sat down to breakfast when they heard the horses and saw the Union soldiers galloping down the street yelling war whoops. Mrs. Ellis recorded, "The roadway was jammed with a surging mass of mounted soldiers and rampant horses spurred to breakneck speed." She continued, "It was frightening, curiously thrilling to see the capless cavalrymen standing erect in their stirrups as they rode, brandishing bared sabers in hand as they let out earsplitting yells."[230]

As Union troops rode through the streets, fighting broke out with retreating Confederates. J.I. Shaver, a young resident of Salisbury, witnessed the skirmish. He wrote, "Mother and I were in the front door when we saw the first of the troopers come through the bridge. These were cavalrymen." As they fought with sabers, he recalled how the Confederate and Federal mounted troops "cut and slashed at each other, cutting up one another right sharp." He witnessed one Confederate officer shoot down two Union troops with his pistol. Shaver later remarked, "Being a youngster I was filled with excitement and ran about all over town."[231]

The Ramsey family, however, was not as excited as young Shaver about the activity in town. Mrs. Maggie Ramsey remembered how "the missiles were flying thick and fast around and upon the house." While watching the fighting from the window, she witnessed a soldier being wounded by a bullet to the back. He was one of the galvanized Irishmen who had not surrendered earlier and was actually fighting. The soldier continued to load and fire his weapon until he reached Mrs. Ramsey's piazza. Although she was alone in the home with her four little children, Mrs. Ramsey refused to let him die without at least trying to assist him in some way. She went out to him and found he had been shot through the lungs. Although she feared the wound was mortal, Mrs. Ramsey sent for a doctor. The soldier said to her, "They have killed me, but I die a brave man; I fought them as long as I could stand." She stayed with him, nursing his wounds as best she could, until help arrived. The doctor was able to remove the bullet, and the soldier was taken to the hospital. Surprisingly, the man survived, and he later returned to thank her for her kindness.[232]

The town of Salisbury was a symbol of hatred among the Union troops, as evidenced by the fierce hand-to-hand street combat. Many of their comrades in arms had perished in the abominable prison camp located in the town. The townspeople, realizing this fact, feared their homes would be looted and burned. Mrs. Ramsey recalled, "Some of the soldiers rushed into the hall and up the steps, demanding of me, 'the damned rebel who lives here,' to make them some coffee and something to eat or else." One cavalryman threatened, "I'll cut you in two!" One Federal officer, after seeing a fine piano in the Ramsey home, demanded her to play a song for him. In her dejected mood, she replied, "I cannot play. There is no music in my soul today."[233]

Mrs. Ellis, however, decided she would make an appeal directly to General Stoneman about the protection of the property of the townspeople. Accompanied by other women, she gained an audience with the general. Reportedly, Stoneman instructed his orderly to show the women in, and when they were announced, the general bowed and touched the brim of his hat. Mrs. Ellis cut straight to the point, saying, "Our personal safety is endangered by the devilish conduct of your looting soldiers." She asked the general to invoke some "civility" upon the soldiers, noting that it would be appreciated among the townspeople. Stoneman, in return, gave strict orders for the protection of the civilians and their property. Other townspeople begged Stoneman not to burn the town, and the general assured them his men would not disturb the property of noncombatants; however, as military necessity, he would destroy any resources and supplies used by the Confederacy.[234]

At Salisbury, Union troops confiscated several warehouses filled with uniforms, blankets, medicine and food, the majority of which had arrived recently from Richmond, Columbia, Charlotte, Danville and Raleigh. As Federal armies threatened these cities, supplies were moved out in an attempt to keep them from falling into Union hands. Stoneman ordered some of the food be distributed to the area's poorer population. The general then gave orders to burn all the warehouses and arsenals. It was observed that "for miles around the locality of the city was marked during the day by a column of dense smoke, and at night by the glare from burning stores." Watching soldiers burn supplies of coffee, bacon and sugar, considered luxury items because of their scarcity at this point in the war, had to be demoralizing to people suffering near starvation for many months.[235]

A primary reason to attack Salisbury was to liberate Federal prisoners. This action was almost anticlimactic since a great majority of the prisoners had been either exchanged or relocated before Stoneman arrived. Only a few inmates, too sick to be transferred, were still being held. Nevertheless, after evacuating the prisoners, Stoneman ordered the buildings to be burned. This brought a feeling of justice, as indicated by Colonel William Palmer when he wrote, "We burned down the infamous Salisbury prison as we came along the way. It is only necessary to see one of these prison lots to know that the suffering has been intentional…You can see murder on the face of it."[236]

The main column moved out of Salisbury that afternoon and headed west toward Statesville, taking prisoners and captured artillery with it. Colonel Palmer's brigade was ordered south to Charlotte to cut the railroad. General Gillem's report of the battle at Salisbury gave special mention to Colonel Miller "for his gallantry at Salisbury, for which I respectfully and earnestly recommend him for the brevet of brigadier-general." He also commended Lieutenant Colonel Stacy "for his uniform gallantry." An ailing Stoneman arrived at Statesville in a carriage around midnight, and soldiers continued to arrive for hours afterward. Word had spread quickly that Stoneman's troops were on the move, so when they arrived, the town was "mostly in the possession of the women and children," as most of the male population packed up food and valuables and hid in the forests.[237] Within a few hours after they occupied the town, they burned Confederate stores, a depot and the offices of the *Iredell Express*, the local newspaper. At this time, General Stoneman believed that he had accomplished all of his objectives. The V&T Railroad had been destroyed, Lee's retreat had been cut off and the prison at Salisbury had been burned. Stoneman planned to return to Knoxville. In his report to General Thomas, Stoneman wrote, "The tithing depots along the route…have furnished us with supplies in the greatest abundance. The number of horses and mules captured and taken along the way I have no means of estimating. I can say we are much better mounted than when we left Knoxville." He continued that the surplus animals were enough "to haul off all of our captures, mount a portion of the prisoners and about a thousand contrabands."[238]

On April 15, they marched in the direction of Lenoir and arrived there on Easter Sunday. They used St. John's Episcopal Church as their headquarters. Colonel Miller was responsible for an estimated nine hundred prisoners, many of whom were sixty years and older, too old for the regular Confederate army. They had walked nearly thirty miles within an eight- to ten-hour period and arrived in poor condition, hungry, fatigued and with blistered feet. General Gillem ordered the guards to shoot anyone who tried to escape, saying he would "rather have ten men shot than one escape."[239] Local families shared what little food they had with the prisoners. One resident, Louisa Norwood, recorded, "Sunday morning we went up to see

General Alvan C. Gillem's staff. Seated from left to right are Major Anthony Carrick (surgeon), General Alvan C. Gillem and Major Sterling Hambright. Standing from left to right are Captain Bayless Miller (brother to Colonel John K. Miller), Lieutenant Obadiah C. French and Captain David M. Nelson (son of Unionist Thomas A.R. Nelson). *Courtesy of the U.S. Army Heritage and Education Center.*

the prisoners…and remember it was Easter Sunday! Of course we paid the poor fellows all the attention we could, taking them all the provisions we could save from the Yanks, and they seemed very grateful." Another witness wrote, "There seemed to be a spirit of bitterness and cruelty toward the prisoners among the men generally, and sometimes the officers." Major

Sterling Hambright, a member of Gillem's staff, apparently went out of his way to mistreat prisoners. For instance, one feeble resident of Lenoir, Dr. J.A. Ballew, was ordered by Major Hambright to march to the church where the other prisoners were being held. When Dr. Ballew did not walk fast enough, Major Hambright walked up behind and gave him "a rousing kick." Dr. Ballew did not survive the imprisonment.[240]

Another prisoner, Major Alphonso C. Avery, who had been captured at Salisbury, was from a very prominent Burke County family. Because of Major Avery's ruthless campaigns, most North Carolina Unionists despised him. In fact, the "home Yankees" in Gillem's command vowed to kill Avery if he was ever captured. Union troops were not aware that Avery had been captured, and with the help of his friend Sidney Deal of Lenoir, he was able to keep his identity a secret. Deal had served as the sheriff of Watauga County when Colonel Miller was sheriff in Carter County. Deal approached Colonel Miller and asked for help in disguising Avery, and probably to his surprise, Miller agreed. Avery was allowed to exchange his Confederate uniform for civilian clothes and trimmed his beard to make him unrecognizable to those who would have certainly killed him. He continued marching along with the other prisoners, eventually ending up at Camp Chase, Ohio. General Gillem admitted the march was difficult, resulting in many deaths along the way, but he adamantly denied an unsubstantiated report that his command had intentionally killed any prisoners.[241]

As the prisoners were marched toward Tennessee, Stoneman departed for Knoxville, leaving General Gillem in full command of the cavalry in order to prevent Confederates from using the mountains and valleys for guerrilla warfare now that the war in Virginia had ended. After the departure of General Stoneman, Gillem encouraged plundering of civilian homes. The local population despised him, describing him as "supercilious, insulting, and unfeeling."[242] Gillem had made known his distaste for Lenoir in particular by referring to it as a "rebellious little hole." At his headquarters, the home of Mr. Albert Hagler, Gillem had the run of the house and had crowded the family into one small room. At one point when General Gillem was ranting to the Haglers about how the Confederates starved the Union prisoners, Mrs. Hagler dared to suggest to Gillem that the suffering could have been avoided had the Federal government agreed to exchange prisoners, sending the Union soldiers north where provisions were plenty. Angry at what he considered her impertinence, Gillem reportedly encouraged his men to plunder the nearby home of Mrs. Hartley, the Haglers' daughter. At the home of Mrs. Hartley, soldiers destroyed virtually everything. They broke open barrels of sorghum and poured it all over the floors of the house and over the wheat in the granary. Her furniture and dishes were smashed, and what was not destroyed was described as being "defiled in a manner so disgusting as to be unfit for use."[243]

The soldiers then turned to the home of Mr. Boone Clark, a disabled Confederate veteran whose wife was also a niece of the Haglers. After chasing Mr. Clark away from the home, the soldiers ransacked the house, "breaking open trunks, wardrobes, drawers" and taking any valuables or weapons they came across. Mrs. Clark and her young daughter were forced to watch, causing Mrs. Clark to break down in a fit of uncontrollable sobbing. Not taking any pity on her at all, the soldiers destroyed the home while shouting insults at her. One soldier grabbed the woman by the throat and struck her as he ripped a gold watch from her neck. She and her daughter managed to escape the house and ran to the home of her aunt, Mrs. Hagler. When asked to intervene, Gillem dismissed the request, merely saying, "There are bad men in all crowds." Not content to leave it at that, Mrs. Hagler demanded that General Gillem provide protection, but he simply turned his back, ignoring her.[244] On the morning of April 17, Gillem's men prepared to move on to their next target: Morganton.

The way to Morganton proved difficult as Gillem discovered the residents were much more defiant. Some eighty Confederate home guardsmen led by Colonel Thomas Walton, Major General John P. McCown and Colonel Samuel McDowell planned out a defense. They destroyed the only bridge that crossed the Catawba River, thus forcing Gillem and his men to cross at a place called Rocky Ford. As the Union forces attempted to ford the river, Walton's men opened fire. The attack forced the Union troops to cross farther down, and they still encountered enemy fire from another group of Confederate guardsmen, made up primarily of seventeen-year-old boys. One of Gillem's men noted that this group "fought with the coolness of veterans." Once the Union troops made it across the river, Walton's men retreated, but the resistance cost Gillem over twenty men wounded and eight killed. This constituted the highest losses on the raid thus far. Because of the resistance, Gillem refused to rein in his men as they ransacked the town. Hardly a home was left untouched by the men as they roamed through the streets taking any possessions they could carry.[245]

Continuing to move west, Gillem planned to use Swannanoa Gap to make an advance on Asheville; however, the gap was blocked by downed trees. Additionally, he encountered Confederate general James G. Martin's five hundred troops with artillery between himself and Asheville. After two days trying to break through, Gillem turned his forces south through Rutherfordton in order to cross the Blue Ridge Mountains and approach Asheville from the south by way of Hendersonville. On April 22, at Hendersonville, Union troops received a report confirming General Lee's surrender to General Grant at Appomattox, Virginia. Additionally, the men were saddened to hear that President Lincoln had been assassinated.[246]

Gillem left Hendersonville the next day, preparing an attack on Asheville the evening of April 23; however, he received a flag of truce from General Martin. Confederate commander General Joseph Johnston and Union general William Sherman issued an armistice as they held peace talks at Durham Station, North Carolina. Gillem and his men camped just south of the town. Vance and Mary Brown, who lived on the road between Hendersonville and Asheville, invited the general and his officers to dinner that evening. Oddly enough, earlier that day Mrs. Brown had recorded, "God grant that we may never live to endure the like again; squads of armed ruffians were coming in and plundering and cursing all night long…thank God my prayers were heard and I escaped untouched, tho' a thousand curses were hurled into my face and I was called a thousand times 'a damned lying rebel.'"[247] Incredibly, due to the truce, Vance Brown, Mary's husband, invited General Gillem and his staff to dinner that same evening. Mrs. Brown wrote, "Little indeed was the sum of all we had to offer…but the best of our little we gave as unto friends, tho' they were all our foes." After dinner, the men relaxed and smoked their pipes while others played cards, as if they had been longtime friends and a war had never taken place. The Browns' daughter, Maria, sang for them, and the band from the Thirteenth Tennessee played "some beautiful old Union pieces." The music continued until after midnight and into the early hours of the next day.[248]

The next day, April 24, General Gillem met with General Martin under a flag of truce, at which time Gillem told him of the decision to march back to Greeneville, Tennessee. Gillem also asked if Martin could supply his troops with three days' rations to avoid "stripping the citizens of their scanty supplies." Martin agreed but asked for the return of his artillery, which had been captured the day before. Gillem refused, reminding Martin that without the armistice "it would have been easy to capture Asheville and its garrison."[249] As Gillem and his men left, the citizens of Asheville breathed a sigh of relief; they were not expecting what came next.

Gillem ordered the Eighth and Thirteenth Cavalry brigades to head for Greeneville, Tennessee. As the war seemed to be over, Gillem had his sights set on a political career. Therefore, after issuing orders to his troops, he took a small escort and left for Nashville. The state legislature was preparing for its first postwar session, and Gillem intended to be there. Nevertheless, that very same day, President Andrew Johnson rejected the peace agreement between Generals Sherman and Johnston. The president and his cabinet accused Sherman of exceeding his orders by providing overly generous terms, including a general amnesty. Sherman was ordered to establish a peace under the same terms as Generals Grant and Lee; in the meantime, he was "ordered to push his military advantages."[250] When word reached General Gillem, he was ten miles north of Asheville. Having been granted a leave of absence to attend the meeting in Nashville, Gillem sent the Eighth and Thirteenth Tennessee division back toward Asheville.[251]

Meanwhile, in Asheville, as Katherine Polk was visiting with friends "discussing the affairs of the day & congratulating ourselves on its peaceful termination," suddenly the sound of galloping horses caught their attention. Polk and her friends were astonished to see "a troop of Yankee Cavalry in hot pursuit of three women. Pistols were fired in quick succession."[252] The very same troops who had departed just twenty-four hours before were now riding wildly through the streets of Asheville. There was no escape this time for the town that at one time was considered a site of the capital of the Confederacy. Just like everyone else, General Martin, who was still in command of the Confederate forces, was taken completely off guard. Martin claimed that he asked General Gillem to give him "forty-eight hours' notice" in case the peace negotiations broke down before resuming hostilities. He maintained that Gillem had agreed to these terms.[253]

William Palmer, recently brevetted general and placed in command at Gillem's departure, sent a letter to General Martin apologizing for the attack. Likewise, Palmer criticized General Simeon Brown for launching the attack on Asheville without orders from him. The letter did not reach General Martin until after his home had been sacked. Martin later wrote, "I have to say that I have heard of no worse plundering any where than was permitted in and near Asheville…I returned to my house in charge of a United States Officer. When we reached the house I found Mrs. Martin and my daughters going over the house with a squad of Federal soldiers holding candles for them to examine all the trunks and for such things as they fancied for themselves." Daniel Ellis, who had been commissioned a captain after the death of William Gourley, remarked he was not surprised that the men of his regiment treated the Confederate civilians of Asheville badly. In his opinion, plundering was justified since many pro-Union families just across the mountains in Tennessee had suffered the same treatment at the hands of Confederate troops. The attack on Asheville, which lasted for two days, marked the official end to Stoneman's raid. General Brown led his troops out of the town with thirty prisoners, including General Martin.[254]

After the attack on Asheville, Captain Ellis was on a special mission into the hills of East Tennessee to rid the region of "rebel scoundrels." Samuel McQueen, who was responsible for some of the worst atrocities against Union residents, was still on the rampage. As the war was coming to a close in April 1865, McQueen tried to escape. He left his home in Johnson County, but as he passed through Ashe County, North Carolina, he was captured. He was brought back to Johnson County and placed under a guard of black soldiers. McQueen, a former slave owner, objected to being guarded by black men and requested a guard of white soldiers. As a result, Ellis and his company were given charge over McQueen. Ellis and his men were ordered to take their prisoner to Taylorsville and turn him over to the jailer. The group had not proceeded very far before one guard, William Hascue Worley, shot McQueen in the back, killing him instantly. Worley was placed under arrest but was never punished for murdering McQueen.[255]

The night that Federal troops returned to Asheville, Confederate president Jefferson Davis was on the run, trying to make it across the Mississippi River by way of South Carolina and Georgia. General Palmer received orders to move through the mountains into South Carolina in an attempt to capture Davis.[256] The Thirteenth Tennessee would accompany Palmer in pursuit of the beleaguered president of the Confederacy.

Chapter 6

"Such Are the Fortunes of War"

The war was winding down, and as news filtered through the ranks that a truce had been established, the men assumed they would return home. Yet they received orders to pursue and capture Confederate president Jefferson Davis along with other high-ranking members of the Confederate government who were trying to escape. Rumor had it that President Davis was traveling with a large sum of gold. So instead of heading toward Tennessee, the regiment crossed into South Carolina on May 1 and made camp. At Anderson, South Carolina, General Palmer and his brigade joined the Tennesseans, and they continued the march toward Athens, Georgia.

The entire force under Palmer reached Athens, Georgia, on the afternoon of May 4, and the Thirteenth Tennessee was ordered to cut the railroad lines to keep Davis from escaping. Just a few days prior to the arrival of Union troops, Confederate brigadier general Alexander W. Reynolds, whose headquarters were located at Athens, had ordered the commissary opened to the general public. While there was not much to offer, the impoverished population took what was left. About the same time, some discharged Confederate soldiers arrived, expecting to receive rations. When they discovered an empty commissary, a near riot ensued, and Union troops restrained the two groups. Yet as the Confederate populace was being restrained, Union raiders, also angry because the commissary was empty, began looting houses and taking provisions from civilians.[257]

The march continued, and after the Thirteenth Tennessee reached Lexington, Georgia, the same day, Lieutenant Colonel Stacy attempted to reprimand some of the soldiers for their latest bout of looting. The men were called to assembly and searched for stolen items. The search turned up twenty-two watches belonging to civilians in Athens. The men were disciplined and the watches returned to their owners. Captain Samuel Scott recorded this episode in the regimental history and noted, "In time of war and the suspension of civil law, there are always some men who do dishonorable acts that bring discredit upon the organization to which they belong."[258] Yet General Palmer was not impressed with the lack of military discipline and requested that the East Tennessee troops be recalled because "their officers for the most part have lost all control over their men. A large number of the men and some of the officers devote themselves exclusively to pillaging and destroying property…they are now so entirely destitute of discipline that it cannot be restored in the field and while the command is living on the country."[259] Yet the East Tennesseans remained part of Palmer's cavalry division, leaving the colonel to deal with circumstances as best he could.

Palmer's command continued to chase President Davis, but it appeared they were always just a step behind. On the morning of May 7, word was received that Davis was about twenty-five miles away in Washington, Georgia. The division started off in that direction. However, before arriving, Palmer received news that Davis had already left and was now traveling southwest on horseback. As Palmer's men continued to pursue Davis, Colonel Miller's brigade was ordered south to Crawfordsville, Georgia, to the home of the Confederate vice president Alexander H. Stephens. Arriving at the home of Stephens, Lieutenant Thomas C. White asked one of the servants to let the vice president know of their presence and to tell him they threatened him in no way. The men asked only for breakfast and corn for the horses. Stephens had been residing at his home for a while now awaiting his fate. He got dressed and went down to speak with the Union soldiers. Stephens recorded in his memoirs that "we talked in a friendly way until breakfast." He continued that Lieutenant Colonel Stacy sent word that he would "be glad to see and take tea with me." To that, Mr. Stephens responded that he would "be glad to see him." That evening, Stacy, along with Adjutant Samuel Angel and Dr. James Cameron, paid a visit to the former vice president. Stephens recorded, "Conversation was agreeable. I invited them to stay all night; they declined but accepted my invitation for breakfast." The men explained to Stephens that they were pursuing President Davis. Three days later, on May 10, Union forces finally caught up with Jefferson Davis, yet the distinction of capturing the Confederate

Alexander H. Stephens served as the vice president of the Confederate States of America. A detachment of the Thirteenth Tennessee led by Colonel John K. Miller arrested Stephens at his home in Crawfordsville, Georgia, on May 11, 1865. He served five months in prison. In 1873, he was elected to the U.S. House of Representatives. He held this position until 1882, when he left to become the governor of Georgia. *Courtesy of the Library of Congress.*

Dr. James Cameron, a Unionist who volunteered with the Thirteenth Tennessee Cavalry despite the fact that he was also a slave owner. After the war, he continued his medical practice in Elizabethton, Tennessee, up until his death in 1897. *Courtesy of Tony Marion.*

president went to the Fourth Michigan Cavalry. The Thirteenth Tennessee returned to Stephens's home and arrested him. He was transported to the military prison at Fort Warren in Boston, Massachusetts.[260]

No longer pressed to capture Davis, Miller's brigade headed for Tennessee but continued to enjoy the hospitality of Southern plantations along the way, whether it was freely offered or not. For instance, the men made the acquaintance of Colonel William McKinley of Milledgeville, Georgia. He was above the age of enlistment during the war but served as colonel of the Governor's Horse Guards. McKinley visited their camps and invited Lieutenant Colonel Stacy and his officers to dinner. Here they were served what was described as "the most elegant and sumptuous dinner we had while soldiering in Dixie." Yet as they moved out early the next morning, they had a different reception from the mistress of a plantation with forty to fifty former slaves "still there and under the strictest discipline." The mistress of the plantation refused to prepare any food for the soldiers. As a result, "necessity overcame our gallantry to the fair sex and an ax answered every purpose of a key." The men carried out hams and bread, asking the servants to cook for them. Captain Scott recorded that no one brought any harm to the mistress for not offering up any food, but she "blessed us in language not found anywhere in the scripture." When the soldiers left the plantation, about a dozen black men left as well.[261]

As it happened, the men were in Greensboro, Georgia, just as the train carrying Jefferson Davis made a stop. Before Davis was transported to Fortress Monroe in Virginia, some members of the regiment were able to

Major Patrick Dyer, a native of Ireland, arrived in New York City in 1853 when he was thirteen years old. He enlisted when the war began and was captured during the First Battle of Manassas in July 1861. He was held at Libby Prison in Richmond, Virginia, and then transferred to the Confederate prison at Salisbury, North Carolina. In 1863, he escaped and traveled into East Tennessee, where he mustered with the Thirteenth Tennessee Cavalry. After the war, he married a young lady from Tennessee and moved first to Missouri and then to Lamar, Texas. He died in 1882. *From Scott and Angel,* History of the Thirteenth Regiment, *facing 96.*

catch a glimpse of the former Confederate president. In an incident repeated many times after the war, Major Patrick Dyer of Company B, a native of Ireland, approached President Davis. Dyer was captured during the First Battle of Manassas in 1861 and confined at Libby Prison in Richmond. Later transferred to the prison at Salisbury, North Carolina, he escaped and made his way into East Tennessee, eventually joining the Thirteenth Tennessee. The major freely addressed Davis, reportedly saying, "Mr. President I am glad to meet you. Probably you do not remember me. When I was at Libby prison I often saw you taking a ride past the prison on a fine white horse. You were at liberty then and I was a prisoner, now you are a prisoner and I am at liberty—such are the fortunes of war—good day Mr. President."[262]

On Stoneman's last raid, the Thirteenth Tennessee marched over one thousand miles, passed through five different states and crossed numerous rivers and mountain ranges. At long last, the regiment had finally made it back to East Tennessee. On June 2, the men arrived at Lenoir's Station, a few miles east of Knoxville. They were anxious to return home to "build up their desolated farms and homes and join their families from whom they had been so long separated." Finally, on September 5, 1865, the officers and men of the Thirteenth Tennessee were paid and mustered out of service. While this was the day they had been waiting for to be "relieved from the restraints of military service," many were sad in departing, and as they shook hands with fellow comrades, many "hearts swelled with emotion."[263]

Colonel Miller suffered much personal loss during the war years. Soon after enlisting with the Union army in 1863, his wife suddenly died, leaving their four children, all under the age of ten, in the care of Miller's elderly in-laws. Additionally, his father-in-law, John Minor, managed the personal property, valued at $1,500 in 1860, while the colonel was away. Confederate home guardsmen took every opportunity while Miller was away to destroy his property. Miller explained that as his home was entirely within enemy lines for most of the war, "as a consequence I have suffered every severity in property matters."[264] As Stoneman's army moved though North Carolina, it conscripted horses, mules and forage from local residents. In return, the owners were given vouchers for the value of the property taken by the soldiers. The holder of the voucher could then redeem the value from the Federal government by visiting a claims office. Since many citizens lived several miles away from the nearest claims office, sometimes it was more convenient to sell the vouchers at a discount to a third-party agent. This person would make an offer on the vouchers and then redeem them for the full amount at the claims offices, thus recovering their investment plus a little extra.[265]

The Dreaded Thirteenth Tennessee Union Cavalry

During the spring of 1865, Colonel Miller found a means to recover some of the monetary losses he had experienced during the war. In early April 1865, as the regiment moved through North Carolina, vouchers were issued to citizens for horses. Miller began buying vouchers from citizens at a discounted rate. However, before engaging in this practice, Miller claimed that he spoke with the quartermaster general to make sure there was no army regulation that prevented officers from buying vouchers. According to Colonel Miller, the quartermaster confirmed there were no restrictions and it would be fine to buy them. By all accounts, Miller was an honest man. His commanding officer, General Alvan Gillem, described him as "one of the most active, energetic, gallant, and competent officers I have ever met either in the volunteer or regular service." Gillem continued that he regarded Miller as "an honorable and high minded gentleman…his character in every way has been above reproach."[266] Furthermore, Miller later testified that he would buy vouchers only from those who were loyalists.

As vouchers were purchased, Miller recorded the transaction in a ledger and then gave the vouchers to Lieutenant Henry A. Kelley, assistant quartermaster, to keep in a haversack. At one point on the raid, the haversack was placed in the charge of an orderly, who subsequently lost it. Miller, not wishing to lose all of his investment, ordered Lieutenant Kelley to take some men and retrace the route with the hopes of finding the haversack. Having retraced the route and seeing no sign of the missing vouchers, the men were about to give up the search when they decided to visit a nearby farmhouse to inquire about the haversack. The woman they spoke with at first denied having it but then finally admitted her children had found it. She went to retrieve the items, and after some time had passed, Lieutenant Kelley walked into the room where the woman had gone and noticed that "the papers were scattered…around the floor. She said the children had been playing with it." The lieutenant, in looking over the receipts, realized that some were missing. Additionally, some of the recovered vouchers were torn and the ink smeared. At this point, Colonel Miller asked Lieutenant Kelley to make out new vouchers based on the ledger he had of the transactions. As they made out new vouchers, Miller claimed he destroyed the old vouchers and believed he had the authority to sign the new vouchers. In issuing new vouchers, four were accidentally duplicated, so when Miller tried to exchange them for payment, he was immediately questioned about the duplicates. On August 8, 1865, by order of General George Stoneman, Colonel John Miller was placed under arrest and held under guard. He was formally indicted on charges of embezzlement and fraud.[267]

Andrew Johnson (circa 1865), a Unionist from Greeneville, Tennessee, remained in the Senate even after the secession of Tennessee. President Lincoln appointed him military governor of Tennessee in March 1862 and then chose him to be his running mate in the presidential election of 1864. After the assassination of President Lincoln in April 1865, Johnson became the seventeenth president of the United States. *Courtesy of the Library of Congress.*

In October 1865, Miller appeared before a general court-marital hearing in Knoxville. Lieutenant Colonel Luther Trowbridge of the Tenth Michigan Cavalry represented Miller at the court-martial. Trowbridge was acquainted with Miller, as he had served in Gillem's First Cavalry Division under General William Palmer during Stoneman's raid. By all accounts, Trowbridge thought highly of Miller, saying he had "a fine reputation as a man of integrity and worth." When the trial ended in November 1865, Colonel Miller was found not guilty to the charge of forgery and counterfeiting; however, he was found guilty on the charge of "conduct to the prejudice of good order and military discipline." Therefore, Miller was dishonorably dismissed from service. Trowbridge immediately appealed the verdict to President Andrew Johnson, writing that a "great wrong and injustice has been done a gallant and meritorious officer." Johnson responded by fully restoring Colonel Miller to his position and rank in the service and ordered that he be honorably discharged.[268] Miller returned home to Elizabethton and assisted in administering oaths of amnesty for former Confederates.

President Andrew Johnson, in May 1865, issued a proclamation offering amnesty to many former Confederates. Upon taking a loyalty oath, a pardon was issued, allowing for restoration of citizenship and property. Nevertheless, high-ranking military and civilian Confederate officials were not eligible under the president's proclamation. In Carter and Johnson Counties, men like John Miller and others from the Thirteenth Tennessee found themselves administering oaths of amnesty. In some cases, members of the Union regiment vouched for the character of former Confederate sympathizers in an attempt to have their citizenship restored. Many applicants who were summoned to court on charges of treason claimed they were only "rebel sympathizers" and had not taken up arms against the Federal government. At times, though, amnesty applicants tried to "split hairs" in terms of their supposed disloyalty to the Union. For instance, Asa Reece from Johnson County testified that he "was only a rebel sympathizer in the late war and took no active part" except for the few weeks when he "bore arms in a home guard company." In an attempt to distinguish how serving with the home guard was different from enlisting with the Confederate army, Reece argued that he took up arms only to suppress "home disorders and not to overthrow the government of the United States."[269]

Other applicants claimed that four years of war had essentially changed their hearts. For instance, Madison T. Peoples had at one time bitterly condemned the Unionists for burning the bridges. At the end of the war, he was indicted for treason, yet surprisingly there were several Union men who came forward to testify on his behalf. Apparently, he had represented many men who had been conscripted by the Confederate army so they would not have to serve. During the war, he had an opportunity to serve as first lieutenant of a Confederate cavalry unit formed in Sullivan County, but he refused the offer. He did not serve in the military for the Confederacy or the Union. Absalom N. McNabb, a Unionist, testified how Peoples on several occasions warned him of approaching Confederate soldiers and how he tried to save the property of Union men. Likewise, when Confederate authorities arrested David Britt as a bushwhacker, Peoples represented him. Britt was released from prison, and all charges were dropped as a result.[270] Daniel Ellis, however, did not think much of him and remarked, "Madison Tennessee Peoples, whose infamous conduct inflicted a foul stigma upon the state whose name he bore." Ellis claimed that Madison and his father, William Peoples, cooperated with home guardsmen such as Vincent Witcher, who routinely reported on loyal families. Even in the amnesty file, Governor "Parson" Brownlow stated, "I have known petitioner from boyhood and have no confidence in the man." Instead, he referred the case to the attorney general, who was also acquainted with Peoples.[271] Nevertheless, Madison Peoples took the oath of allegiance and was pardoned.

Marauding Mountain Men

At times, it seemed that residents tried to make the best of a bad situation. Isaac E. Wilson, of Johnson County, wrote that he never voted for "separation" from the Union; however, after Tennessee seceded, he was elected sheriff. As the Confederate government passed the conscription law, Wilson was held accountable to enforcing the law. In his petition for amnesty, he pointed out that he was elected during a time when "the citizens of the county were without any aid from the federal government" and he only accepted the position to protect the loyal people of the county.[272] Likewise, George Shults of Cocke County claimed he was always a Unionist and even took "repeated beatings" from the Confederate home guard for his loyalty to the Federal government. Yet, as he was elected justice of the peace for his county, he took the oath of office under the "rebel government." By the end of the war, Shults was "living in exile from his home."[273]

Other petitioners testified that while they did not vote for separation, once the state of Tennessee left the Union, they felt compelled to support the wishes of the people. Some well-to-do families of Carter County were split in their loyalties for the Union and the Confederacy. After the war, many veterans from the Thirteenth Tennessee came forward and vouched for their good character. For instance, Isaac P. Tipton was an elderly farmer who submitted his petition for amnesty explaining that he voted against separation and never served in the Confederate army. He had two sons who served in the Confederate army, neither of whom survived the war. Colonel Miller administered the oath and signed a petition, along with many other Unionists, endorsing Tipton as a "good citizen."[274]

Additionally, the Taylor family of Carter County was well respected. George, Henry and Nat Taylor all served with the Confederate military. Their uncle was Nathaniel Taylor, an outspoken Unionist who traveled throughout the North during the war raising money for the East Tennessee Relief Association. All three men survived the war and took the amnesty oath. George testified that he had voted against separation but when Tennessee seceded he was forced to enlist under the conscription act. Henry explained that he was a college student at Chapel Hill, North Carolina, when the war began. He enlisted under the conscription act but spent most of the war as a prisoner at Johnson's Island in Ohio. Finally, Nat Taylor testified that he voted against secession but when Tennessee seceded he "acquiesced in what then seemed to be the action of a majority of her citizens." He claimed never to have fired a weapon, nor was he ever in active service against the Union. During the war, these men had used their influence with Confederate officials to protect Union men and property. After the war, the favor was returned, as Union men testified on their behalf.[275]

Sometimes events that occurred during the war led to an amicable relationship after the war between former Unionists and Confederates. Major Henderson M. Folsom served as quartermaster for the Sixty-ninth North Carolina Confederate regiment, also known as Thomas's Legion. Thomas's Legion was despised in the region because two of its companies were made up of Cherokee Indians. During the war, Major Folsom had taken steps in allowing the Heatherly family, who were Unionists, to retrieve and bury the body of Thomas Heatherly Jr. Heatherly had been executed by Confederate captain B.H. Duvall in retaliation for the murders of Robert Tipton and William Brooks. Yet Folsom's act of kindness to the Heatherly family resonated with the rest of the Unionist community. Because Folsom was a major, he was ineligible for a pardon. Several members of the Thirteenth Tennessee living in Carter and Johnson Counties after the war drew up a petition asking President Johnson to consider a special pardon for Folsom. They declared that during the war he had used his influence as much as possible to shield Unionist families.[276]

After the war, Roderick Butler resumed his congressional career as well as his law practice. Butler assisted in many pension requests made after the war, particularly widow's pensions. There were on some occasions questions of loyalty on the part of the petitioners. For instance, in the case of Amanda E. Vaught, several residents of Johnson County testified that she was undeserving of a pension because she had been openly disloyal during the war. Her husband, George W. Vaught, had enlisted as a sergeant with Company M of the Thirteenth Tennessee in February 1864. Prior to that time, he had hidden out in the surrounding mountains in an effort to avoid the Confederate conscription officers. According to the testimony, Amanda Vaught along with her family, the Naffs, openly sided with the Confederacy. In fact, she was described as "one of the bitterest rebels" in the county, doing everything she could to aid the Southern cause. Samuel Forrester testified that when George Vaught was hiding in the mountains, his wife asked where he was hiding. Forrester said he knew better than to tell her because she would have turned him in to the Confederate authorities. When Forrester told Mrs. Vaught he did not know where her husband was, she reportedly remarked, "If he likes the Yankees better than me then I hope I never lay eyes on him again!" As it happened, she never did lay eyes on him again. Sergeant Vaught was wounded in the leg during the Bulls Gap stampede. His leg was amputated, but he died nevertheless at a private residence on

Congressman Roderick R. Butler (circa 1875) served in the U.S. House of Representatives from 1867 to 1875 and then again from 1887 to 1889. Butler represented Tennessee's First District and assisted many veterans and widows of veterans from the Thirteenth Tennessee Cavalry in securing war pensions. *From the Barnes Photographic Collection: Box 2 Folder 60, Georgetown University Library Special Collections Research Center, Washington, D.C.*

Private Frederick Shoun, from Johnson County, Tennessee, who enlisted with Company B. *Courtesy of Tony Marion.*

November 26, 1864. Vaught left behind two children, both under the age of ten. When Amanda Vaught submitted her widow's pension application, G.H. Ragsdale, a special agent, was assigned to investigate the case. Ragsdale concluded that while the evidence was overwhelming that Amanda Vaught was a Confederate sympathizer, she did not actively assist the Confederate government, and he did not wish to deprive the children of their father's pension. Therefore, she was awarded eight dollars a month, along with two dollars per child each month until their sixteenth birthdays.[277]

The postwar years witnessed former adversaries working together in order to rebuild their lives and communities. The experience of war had changed them forever. In the words of Civil War veteran and Supreme Court justice Oliver Wendell Holmes, "The generation that carried on the war has been set apart by its experience…in our youth our hearts were touched with fire."[278] Because their generation had been set apart by the experience of war, veterans of the Thirteenth Tennessee worked not only to rebuild their lives but also to build a legacy for their children and grandchildren. They sought to be a revered part of Tennessee's history and be remembered as courageous soldiers who bravely served their country and not as lawless marauders.

Chapter 7

"THEIR GLORY SHALL NOT BE BLOTTED OUT"

Memorialization during the postwar years played an important role in honoring Civil War veterans. Reunions and monument ceremonies gave Union and Confederate veterans a chance to keep their identity alive and, more importantly, impart to a younger generation the meaning of service and sacrifice. Major William McKinley, also a veteran of the late war, understood the experience of war and the importance it played in the minds of veterans as he campaigned for the presidency in 1896. When a delegation of more than five hundred East Tennesseans traveled to Canton, Ohio, to pay a visit to the Republican presidential hopeful, McKinley took the opportunity to praise the East Tennesseans for their loyalty. Not always known for his oratory skills when compared to his Democratic rival William Jennings Bryan, McKinley nonetheless delivered a rousing speech, during which he commended Tennessee for its "splendid patriots, statesmen, and upright servants." He noted that East Tennesseans in particular had participated in pivotal points throughout history. He called to mind the gallantry of John Sevier and of their ancestors who marched to Kings Mountain during the American Revolution, the great victory of Andrew Jackson at the Battle of New Orleans during the War of 1812 and the bravery and sacrifice of East Tennesseans with their decided stance for the Union during the Civil War. In response to these heroic images, the crowd gave three cheers "for the next President."[279]

Just a few weeks prior to the presidential election, the Thirteenth Tennessee Cavalry Association organized its first veterans' reunion.

Newspaper announcements invited veterans and their families to gather at Butler, Tennessee, for a two-day reunion. The *Elizabethton Mountaineer* publicized the soldiers' reunion as one of the most interesting events of the year. It was fitting that the first reunion be held in the town of Butler. Prior to the Civil War, the town was called Smith's Mill after one of the first settlers, Ezekiel Smith. After the war, it was renamed in honor of Lieutenant Colonel Roderick Butler. The organizers promised music, singing and a time of reminiscing around the campfire. More than 1,500 veterans and their families converged on Butler during the two days. The veterans assembled in front of the Curtis-Farthing store and marched down Main Street with great fanfare as the Butler Band led the way. After reaching the campus of the Watauga Academy, the men broke ranks and were welcomed by the president of the academy, Professor James H. Smith. As the veterans and their families enjoyed a leisurely picnic lunch on the campus grounds, Samuel Scott introduced the keynote speaker, Judge Newton Hacker, a former captain with the Fourth Tennessee Infantry. In his remarks, Judge Hacker paid high tribute to the dedication and patriotism of loyal East Tennesseans and called special attention to their "heroic courage and unfaltering devotion" for the Union cause.[280]

There was quite a bit of embellishing at the reunion as stories were told around the campfire. Dr. Lawson Hyder attended the 1896 reunion and relished the opportunity to share his comical Christmas escape in 1861. He and some other men were charged with bridge burning and were going to be shot on Christmas Day. Because the jail was full, the men were held under guard at the home of William Hawkins. Determined not to see Hyder and the others executed, several young ladies organized a Christmas party at the Hawkinses' home and, of course, invited the Confederate guards. To celebrate the festivities, copious amounts of apple brandy were served, and the girls then persuaded the solders to dance. The drinking, singing and dancing lasted just long enough to allow the Union prisoners to make their escape.[281] Likewise, Corporal Henry Lineback offered his story about the day he enlisted. Lineback, who was just fifteen years old when he enlisted, said he stood on a box to make himself look as tall as the others. He claimed that the mustering officer either took no notice or just did not care.[282]

During the second day of the reunion, thoughts turned to those who had been killed during the war or who had passed away since the end of the war. Reportedly, it was an emotional time as Reverend E.H. Hicks offered a prayer of thanksgiving for those who gave their lives and for the families left behind. After the prayer, the men sang "Nearer My God to Thee," and

Reunion photo of the Thirteenth Tennessee Cavalry. Note the two gentlemen sitting at the center of the photograph. In the second row, seated ninth from the left holding a cane, is Samuel Angel, and the gentleman to his left is Samuel Scott. Also note the African American gentleman standing on the far left of the photograph. This is William Taylor, a former slave who joined the regiment as a cook. After the war, he was awarded a pension for his military service. *Courtesy of Joyce M. Schellenger.*

the band struck up some patriotic tunes. Before departing, the men gathered for a group photo, a tradition that continued at future reunions. In fact, the first reunion was so successful that veterans continued to gather every year for nearly thirty years.[283]

In the following years, the Thirteenth Tennessee Cavalry Association took on other roles besides organizing annual reunions. It assisted fellow comrades in securing military pensions, took steps to record a regimental history to preserve the legacy for future generations and continually deflected allegations of misconduct by the regiment, particularly when it involved the circumstances of John Hunt Morgan's death.

The veterans believed their defining moment came in killing the flamboyant Confederate cavalryman, General John Hunt Morgan. Samuel Scott and Samuel Angel later wrote in the regimental history, "This was the first fight of importance…The officers and men showed the gallantry…of veterans." Further, they contended, the "conspicuous part" played by the regiment in the death of Morgan won them "distinction."[284] Southern Confederates nevertheless insisted that Morgan's death came as

THE DREADED THIRTEENTH TENNESSEE UNION CAVALRY

Above: Reunion photo of the Thirteenth Tennessee Cavalry. *Courtesy of Joyce M. Schellenger.*

Left: Confederate general John H. Morgan. *Courtesy of the Tennessee State Library and Archives, Nashville, T.N.*

a result of an unfair fight, while others alleged it was nothing short of murder. After the war, these viewpoints became meshed with Lost Cause rhetoric, elevating Morgan's image to that of folk hero while veterans of the Thirteenth Tennessee were depicted as gratuitous bushwhackers who had perpetuated an atrocity.

As allegations of misconduct continued to surface during the postwar years, veterans went on the defensive. In a fiery letter to the editor of the *Jonesboro Union Flag,* Christopher C. Wilcox, who had been promoted to major in the latter days of the war, responded to charges of "uncivilized and inhuman treatment toward prisoners of war." Wilcox, who commanded the detachment responsible for Morgan's death, fiercely defended the actions of his men, insisting they were among "the best and most loyal men" of the regiment. Writing with an almost exasperated tone, Wilcox affirmed that Morgan was shot while trying to make an escape. Further, he insisted that accusations of murder were "as base as hell, and as dark and damning as midnight." He claimed the minds of readers had been "poisoned" by the printing of such lies and believed those spreading falsehoods were "devoid of all honor and principle and not worth to occupy the most dismal cell in our State or National prisons."[285]

General Gillem attempted, at least on one occasion, to set the record straight. In a February 1869 letter to William H. Sneed, former U.S. congressman and Knoxville lawyer, Gillem reiterated the details from his official report surrounding Morgan's death. In the letter, Gillem identified Jimmy Leedy as his informant and ardently denied that any member of Mrs. Williams's household passed information to him. He called charges of murder "groundless," maintaining that Private Campbell was at least eighty yards away and had no indication that the man he had shot was Morgan. Finally, he insisted that the general's body "was properly cared for by the captured members of his [Morgan's] staff, aided by my own staff."[286] A few years later, General Gillem's chief of staff, Colonel J.W. Scully, added to Gillem's account, stating that Morgan's body was never paraded up and down the street nor was it left at the train depot. He also noted that Captain Rogers of Morgan's staff was his guest for more than a week after his capture. Scully affirmed that Rogers "spoke in the highest terms of the manner in which they were treated."[287]

Yet veterans continued their efforts to establish the actual details of their 1864 raid on Greeneville. In 1902, three members of Company G—John Wilcox, John Burchfield and William Bishop—made sworn statements concerning the death of Morgan and placed the affidavits on file at the

Crayon image of John and Thomas Burchfield of Company B. *Courtesy of Tennessee State Library and Archives, Nashville, TN.*

Carter County Courthouse. All three men were eyewitnesses to the event, and their statements refuted the idea that General Morgan was unarmed, had surrendered at the time of his death and that Union soldiers had ignored his pleas for mercy and shot him without cause. Additionally, all three swore that Morgan was dead when they carried him to Campbell's horse and that there was "no indignity" inflicted on the body. In particular, Burchfield remembered, Captain Christopher Wilcox examined Morgan's Colt pistols and verified that each chamber had been snapped.[288]

Additionally, the Thirteenth Tennessee Cavalry Association was concerned with "false and slanderous" information written in school textbooks.[289] When Tennessee schools adopted Susan P. Lee's *Advanced School History of the United States* (1895), the veterans mounted a successful protest campaign. The book perpetuated the story of betrayal, murder and misconduct in the death of Morgan. Lee claimed that Morgan was unarmed and had surrendered when "a cavalryman rode up within two feet of him…shot and killed him, and afterwards inflicted indignities upon his dead body."[290] John Wilcox, a veteran of the Thirteenth Tennessee and son of Christopher Wilcox, responded in an editorial, saying that when "false and slanderous imputations assume the form of school history…we arise with one voice to denounce it as false, and to say it shall not be taught to our children."[291] The battle against the textbook's version of the story continued with Alexander B. Wilson's 1902 *National Tribune* article. Wilson, a lawyer by profession, argued, "It would be discreditable to the publisher of any respectable political newspaper at the present time to publish them as facts. How much worse is the offense when they are published as facts in a school book."[292] Because of these and other efforts, the unfounded details of Morgan's death were removed from later editions of Lee's book.

As the years passed, Colonel Miller remained a revered member of the community and was held up as a true hero who had assembled this diverse group of men. The *Greeneville New Era* paid tribute to Miller, writing, "His record as an officer and a patriot is without reproach."[293] After the war, Miller lived in Johnson City, Tennessee, and owned a hotel and general store. He also tried his hand at politics and was elected a senator in Tennessee's General Assembly, serving from 1879 to 1881.[294] The former colonel attended the first few reunions, but failing health kept him from later gatherings. Yet he was never far from the minds of the men, and in one reunion photograph, veterans held a portrait of the revered colonel. He passed away at his home in Carter County, Tennessee, on July 10, 1903, at the age of seventy-six. Many comrades attended the funeral to pay their last respects to their colonel.[295]

Reunion photo of the Thirteenth Tennessee Cavalry. Note the portrait of Colonel John K. Miller being displayed. *Courtesy of Joyce M. Schellenger.*

The Dreaded Thirteenth Tennessee Union Cavalry

Reunion photo of the Thirteenth Tennessee Cavalry. Note the flag provided by R.R. Butler. *Courtesy of Joyce M. Schellenger.*

Unfortunately, Roderick Butler was also too feeble in later years to attend the veterans' reunions, but he always managed to send a note of appreciation to his loyal friends and comrades. The men always remembered how Colonel Butler had used his influence to ease the suffering of East Tennesseans. Every year after the reunion, many veterans in a show of gratitude visited Butler's home to shake his hand. Before his death, he was nearly blind, but he still sat on the front porch as veterans filed by one by one, each speaking a word of thanks. Colonel Butler died at his home in August 1902, and when the reunion was held that year, veterans posed with an American flag bearing the name of the Honorable R.R. Butler.[296]

Many of the men remembered with fondness the character of Lieutenant Colonel William H. Ingerton. They held him in such high regard as an officer and gentleman. Admittedly, they had lost contact with Ingerton's wife after the sad episode resulting in the colonel's death in Knoxville at the hands of a vengeful assassin. After inflicting the mortal wound to Ingerton, the assassin, Joshua Walker, was arrested, but he had escaped, never standing trial for the murder. After the war, the men learned that Walker had returned to his home in Sevier County, Tennessee, and was killed in 1892 when he fell from his wagon and was dragged to death by the horses. He was reportedly intoxicated at the time of the accident.[297] Upon hearing this, veterans of the Thirteenth Tennessee took great satisfaction that the debt had finally been repaid.

While Ingerton's military career was beyond reproach, it appears that his personal life was a mess, a fact that did not become apparent until after his death. Before the war, Ingerton was a second lieutenant with the Sixteenth U.S. Infantry stationed at Fort Walla Walla in the Washington Territory. There he met Anna McCarthy Mayo, a washerwoman for the soldiers at the fort. Anna was originally from Philadelphia and married to Carter H. Mayo, also a soldier stationed in the Washington Territory. The couple had a two-year-old daughter named Clara. By the time William Ingerton met Anna, she was in a desperate situation, as her husband had been discharged from the army and subsequently had abandoned her and the child. At this time, a relationship ensued between Anna and William. She secured a divorce on October 1, 1860, on grounds of abandonment, and a few short weeks later, on October 28, Anna and William were married in Vancouver, Washington.[298]

In May 1861, a month after the first shots of the Civil War were fired at Fort Sumter, Ingerton was transferred to Illinois. Anna, now three months pregnant with the couple's first child, returned with young Clara to Philadelphia. In the meantime, William was moved to Camp Thomas at Columbus, Ohio. As Ingerton was a native of Ohio, it is highly probable that he visited his relatives living near Dayton. At this time, he also made the acquaintance of a twenty-two-year-old young lady named Martha "Mattie" Sargent, who was studying at the nearby Southwestern Normal School to become a teacher.[299] The two undoubtedly struck up a friendship and remained in touch as the war progressed. Apparently, Ingerton did not share with Mattie the fact that he was already married and that his wife was expecting a baby soon. In November, Ingerton received orders sending him to Camp Wood in Kentucky. The transfer came about the same time as he received news that Anna had given birth to a stillborn baby. He traveled to Philadelphia to be with his wife and to arrange the burial of their infant son on November 26, 1861.[300]

The war and long separations apparently took their toll on the Ingerton marriage. In a letter that Ingerton wrote to his wife in April 1864, just before taking command of the Thirteenth Tennessee, there is evidence to suggest that they had been arguing. In an effort to make up with Anna, he wrote, "I cannot afford to lose you for you are my only hope for happiness." He reminded her of his "petulant temper" and that she should overlook the times when he "scolds" her and wrote "bad letters" to her.[301]

Also in this letter, there is a hint of aggravation on the part of Ingerton. Although he tells his wife that "I am coming to see you my love," he continues that "it is very hard that you don't have any money" and because he has not been paid he will have to "borrow money" to come to Philadelphia.[302] At this time, Anna was pregnant again and due to give birth in June. Ingerton came to Philadelphia to be with his wife until he was appointed lieutenant colonel of the Thirteenth Tennessee in May 1864. This would be the last time Anna would see her husband, and she would soon learn of his secret relationship with Mattie Sargent.

In May 1864, Ingerton joined the Thirteenth Tennessee in Gallatin, Tennessee, to take command. As Ingerton settled into his new command, Anna gave birth the next month to a healthy daughter. At the same time, Ingerton continued his relationship with Mattie, eventually proposing marriage. The couple was married on July 31, 1864, at the home of Mattie's sister in Champaign County, Ohio.[303] Mattie accompanied her new husband back to Gallatin, where she remained at his headquarters. When the regiment was ordered to East Tennessee, Colonel Ingerton assigned Captain Scott to escort Mrs. Ingerton across the mountains in her wagon. Captain Scott remarked later that she "was highly educated and most intelligent and agreeable lady."[304]

Mattie was with her husband the night he was shot by Walker at Knoxville. For two weeks, she remained by his side, nursing him until he died on December 8, 1864. Lieutenant Colonel Jacob Thornburg of the Fourth Tennessee Cavalry and his wife, Ada, also witnessed the tragedy at Franklin House. Mrs. Thornburg in a letter to her cousin remarked, "Col. Ingerton… died this eve about dark. His poor wife is here. They have only been married five or six months. She is a poor delicate woman. I do feel so sorry for her. The officers & soldiers…greatly mourn the loss of so good an officer."[305]

It is not entirely clear when Anna Ingerton was notified of her husband's death, since the body was released to Mattie, who traveled back with it to Ohio for burial. Funeral services were held for Ingerton in Champaign, Ohio, where he was laid to rest. By this time, Mattie was aware that she was carrying Ingerton's child, a son born in May 1865 and named William Henry Ingerton in honor of his father. In the meantime, both Anna and Mattie applied for a widow's pension. It was at this point in time that the women discovered each other. After some delay in sorting out all the details, in January 1866, Anna was awarded a pension amounting to thirty dollars a month, as it was determined that she was the legal wife of William Ingerton. Anna Ingerton lost the last connection to her husband when their daughter died in April 1866, just two months shy of her second birthday. Anna remained in Philadelphia until her death in 1898. Oddly enough, when Anna Ingerton died, the pension passed to her daughter, Clara Mayo. Clara was from Anna's first marriage and not the biological daughter of William Ingerton. Meanwhile, Mattie never remarried, nor did she drop the Ingerton name. William Ingerton's son, his only biological child, never received any of his pension money. In order to make a living for herself and her son, Mattie moved from Ohio in 1869 to Newark, New Jersey, where she taught school at a foster home for children for a few years. When William was ten years old, they moved to Texas, where Mattie again taught school to earn a living. In the 1880s, they moved to Amarillo, where she served as a school principal and then later was appointed postmaster. Mattie remained in Amarillo until her death in 1895. Her son, William, became a successful rancher and businessman in Texas.[306]

The war also brought men together who otherwise may have never met and created a strong bond of comradeship. Lieutenant Colonel B.P. Stacy and Captain Samuel Angel forged a strong friendship that lasted much longer than the war. After the war, Stacy and Angel married sisters, Margaret and Julia Piper, respectively, in a double ceremony. They also went into the mercantile business together in Knoxville, Tennessee. Unfortunately, Stacy suffered from declining health in the years after the war. In 1880, Stacy and his wife relocated to Texas, hoping the climate would be an improvement for his health.[307] His health further deteriorated, and his wife took him back to Knoxville to die. Angel moved Stacy

Adjutant Samuel P. Angel, native of Elizabethton, Tennessee, and co-author of the regimental history of the Thirteenth Tennessee. He served as adjutant and commissary of the regiment until the end of the war. After the war, he and Lieutenant Colonel B.P. Stacy married sisters and went into the mercantile business together in Knoxville, Tennessee. He died in Knoxville in 1907. *From Scott and Angel*, History of the Thirteenth Regiment, *facing 48*.

into his own home and remained at the side of his old comrade and business partner until Stacy's death in September 1882. In the eulogy, Angel said of his friend, "He was not only brave but warmhearted and true, making friends of soldiers and citizens alike."[308]

Some veterans moved away from East Tennessee in an attempt to put the war behind them, but ironically, many found themselves coming back to the old homeplace. John Burchfield moved first to Illinois, then to Kansas and then to Washington, D.C., where he became a member of the Capitol Police. Finally, he returned to Elizabethton and took a position as chief engineer at the Mountain Branch of the National Soldiers' Home for Disabled Veterans at Johnson City, known locally as Mountain Home.[309] Burchfield's old friend Samuel Scott also moved away only to return in later years. Scott suffered from failing health and was treated at Mountain Home. During the Butler, Tennessee reunion, Scott was elected regimental historian, but ill health delayed the writing of the history. In 1901, Scott enlisted the help of his longtime friend Samuel Angel to help in the task of writing the history of the Thirteenth Tennessee. After interviewing hundreds of individuals, the manuscript was finally published in 1903.[310]

Members of the Thirteenth Tennessee Cavalry Association continually pressed for a monument to honor the regiment. By 1904, plans were made to construct a monument that would honor all Civil War veterans by placing a Confederate and Union soldier at the top shaking hands. John J. McCorkle, Thirteenth Tennessee veteran and a member of the building committee, explained that having soldiers from either side "clasping hands" promoted

THE DREADED THIRTEENTH TENNESSEE UNION CAVALRY

Reunion photo of the Thirteenth Tennessee Cavalry. *Courtesy of Joyce M. Schellenger.*

unity and that "we are a united country all striving for the same ideals."[311] However, the project was continually delayed due to a lack of funding. Construction finally began in 1912, but the original monument design was replaced with plans for a sixty-five-foot obelisk constructed of river rock and cement at an estimated cost of $3,500. By the time construction began, the building committee, along with Elizabethton mayor C.F. Carrier, had decided the monument should represent all soldiers from the American Revolution to 1912, rather than just Civil War soldiers. The monument was dedicated on October 10, 1913, and coincided with the annual veterans' reunion. Veterans and area citizens proudly gathered in Elizabethton to unveil a simple obelisk in a shared honor of all veterans since the American Revolution.[312]

Meanwhile, in Kentucky a few years earlier, the United Daughters of the Confederacy (UDC) proposed a $15,000 monument to honor the memory of John Hunt Morgan. Ironically, Morgan and his men had used "slash-and-burn tactics" on citizens in Kentucky with little regard for wartime rules of chivalry that his admirers bestowed on him. During the postwar years, Morgan was compared to Robin Hood, and he and his men were credited with seeking to liberate Kentucky, a state that had rejected secession, from "enemy occupation." The United Daughters of the Confederacy raised half the funds to build the monument, while the Kentucky State Senate appropriated the remainder. In October 1911, a great ceremony was held in the courthouse square at Lexington, Kentucky, to mark the unveiling of

Above: Soldiers' monument dedication (1913), Elizabethton, Tennessee. *Courtesy of Tennessee State Library and Archives, Nashville, TN.*

Right: Sergeant John J. McCorkle participated in what was called the Carter County rebellion in the days after the bridge burning in late 1861. He was only fifteen years old at the time. He enlisted with the Thirteenth Tennessee at age seventeen and remained with the regiment until promoted to lieutenant of the First U.S. Colored Heavy Artillery in early 1865. After the war, he was one of the driving forces behind building a monument in Elizabethton, Tennessee, to honor Civil War veterans. *Courtesy of Cheryl Clark.*

The Dreaded Thirteenth Tennessee Union Cavalry

Reunion photo of the Thirteenth Tennessee Cavalry. This photo was taken in the early twentieth century on the steps of the Carter County Courthouse in Elizabethton, Tennessee. *Courtesy of the Archives of Appalachia, East Tennessee State University, Johnson City, TN.*

Morgan's equestrian statue. Surviving members of Morgan's command, along with thousands of admirers, turned out for the special occasion.[313] The unveiling of the statue was met with loud applause and celebration for a man who had brought much destruction to their state.

Morgan's body was interred three different times before finally being placed in a family plot in Lexington, Kentucky. Each one was marked with a lavish ceremony. In contrast, Andrew Campbell, the man credited with Morgan's death, died almost penniless and virtually unknown. He was denied a military pension after several appeals, including one made directly to President Benjamin Harrison. Mrs. Henrietta Gauntlett, Campbell's neighbor, in 1891 wrote to the president detailing Campbell's service to his country and the role he played in Morgan's death. Campbell never received a pension. He died in St. Louis, Missouri, on June 11, 1894, and was buried in a pauper's grave.[314]

The veterans of the Thirteenth Tennessee held reunions every year, but their numbers continued to dwindle. By 1924, only 30 members were able to attend the reunion. In all, only about 60 veterans remained of the original

Monument to General John H. Morgan (circa 1911), dedicated in Lexington, Kentucky, by the United Daughters of the Confederacy. Thousands of people turned out to witness the unveiling of the $15,000 monument. *Courtesy of the Library of Congress.*

1,400 men who served with the regiment.[315] Just as the young men of the Thirteenth Tennessee looked to their forefathers for inspiration, a new and younger generation was now left to evaluate their importance in history and, in doing so, could apply the following scriptural quote:

> *Let us now praise famous men, and our fathers that begat us…All these were honored in their generations, and were the glory of their times. There be of them that have left a name behind them, that their praises might be reported. And some there be, which have no memorial; who are perished, as though they had never been; and are become as though they had never been born; and their children after them…Their seed shall remain forever, and their glory shall not be blotted out.*[316]

Notes

Introduction

1. Thomas G. Burton–Ambrose N. Manning Collection, Series 8: Field Recordings, Audio Tapes 73, 81. Archives of Appalachia, East Tennessee State University, Johnson City, Tennessee.
2. James Alex Baggett, *Homegrown Yankees: Tennessee's Union Cavalry in the Civil War* (Baton Rouge: Louisiana State University Press, 2009), 1.
3. H.K. Weand, "Our Last Campaign and Pursuit of Jeff Davis," in *History of the Fifteenth Pennsylvania Volunteer Cavalry*, ed. Charles H. Kirk (Philadelphia, 1906), 523.
4. Robert E. Corlew, *Tennessee: A Short History* (Knoxville: University of Tennessee Press, 1981), 3.
5. Theodore Roosevelt, *The Winning of the West, Volume I: From the Alleghenies to the Mississippi, 1796–1776* (New York: G.P. Putnam's Sons, 1889), 168.
6. Oliver P. Temple, *East Tennessee and the Civil War* (1899; repr., Johnson City, 1995), 5–7.
7. Temple, *East Tennessee and the Civil War*, 18–40; Thomas William Humes, *The Loyal Mountaineers of Tennessee* (Knoxville, TN, 1888), 43–56.
8. According to the 1860 U.S. census, East Tennessee had a total slave population of 27,539, while Middle Tennessee had 148,382 slaves and West Tennessee had 97,113 slaves.
9. Eric Russell Lacy, *Vanquished Volunteers: East Tennessee Sectionalism from Statehood to Secession* (Johnson City, TN, 1965), 169, 170; Noel C. Fisher, *War at Every Door: Partisan Politics and Guerrilla Violence in East Tennessee, 1860–1869* (Chapel Hill, NC, 1997), 11, 22; Temple, *East Tennessee and the Civil War*, 122–31.
10. John C. Inscoe, *Race, War, and Remembrance in the Appalachian South* (Lexington, KY, 2008), 111; Robert Tracy McKenzie, *Lincolnites and Rebels: A Divided Town in the American Civil War* (New York, 2006), 63.

11. Samuel W. Scott and Samuel P. Angel, *History of the Thirteenth Regiment Tennessee Volunteer Cavalry, U.S.A.* (1903; repr., Johnson City, 1987), 16, 111–13; Temple, *East Tennessee and the Civil War*, 364–65.
12. Many of the men who made up the ranks of the Thirteenth Tennessee Volunteer Cavalry were from Carter and Johnson Counties; however, there were recruits from Washington, Sullivan and Greene Counties in Tennessee and Ashe, Mitchell, Watauga and Wilkes Counties in North Carolina.
13. Scott and Angel, *History of the Thirteenth Regiment*, 258, 259.
14. Edward McCook as quoted in William R. Carter, *History of the First Regiment of Tennessee Volunteer Cavalry in the Great War of the Rebellion* (Knoxville, TN, 1902), 334–35.
15. United States War Department, *The War of the Rebellion: A Compilation of the Official Records of the Union and Confederate Armies* (Washington, D.C., 1880–1901), Series I, Vol. 16 (2), 909–10 (hereinafter *OR*).

Chapter 1

16. Lacy, *Vanquished Volunteers*, 218. Majorities in every East Tennessee county opposed the convention with the exception of Sullivan and Meigs.
17. Order of secession was as follows: South Carolina on December 20, 1860; Mississippi on January 9, 1861; Florida on January 10, 1861; Alabama on January 11, 1861; Georgia on January 19, 1861; Louisiana on January 26, 1861; Texas on February 1, 1861. After the fight at Fort Sumter, the following Southern states passed ordinances of secession: Virginia on April 17, 1861; Arkansas on May 6, 1861; North Carolina on May 20, 1861; and Tennessee on June 8, 1861.
18. *Washington Evening Times*, "Stirring Adventures of Mr. John G. Burchfield during the Civil War," June 18, 1902.
19. *OR* III, 1, 81.
20. Charles F. Bryan Jr., "A Gathering of Tories: The East Tennessee Convention of 1861," *Tennessee Historical Quarterly* 34 (1980): 35, 38; Scott and Angel, *History of the Thirteenth Regiment*, 38, 39.
21. Deposition of Frederick Slimp, December 31, 1867, in *Papers in the Case of J. Powell v. R.R. Butler*, 40th Cong., 2nd sess., H. Misc. Doc. 28, 50.
22. Scott and Angel, *History of the Thirteenth Regiment*, 403.
23. *Knoxville Whig*, May 11, May 25, June 1, 1861.
24. Temple, *East Tennessee and the Civil War*, 80–90, 160–63, 180–85, 192–209; *Proceedings of the E.T. Convention: Held at Knoxville, May 30th and 31st, 1861 and at Greeneville on the 17th Day of June, 1861, and Following Days* (Knoxville, TN: H. Barry's Book and Job Office, 1861), 10.
25. Lacy, *Vanquished Volunteers*, 217–33. Of the thirty counties in East Tennessee, only Sullivan, Meigs, Monroe, Rhea, Sequatchie and Polk voted in favor of secession. The percent voting against secession was most heavy in the counties where Whigs had been traditionally strong, including Sevier (96 percent against), Carter (94 percent against), Campbell (94 percent against) and Anderson (93 percent against). Counties voting for secession all traditionally supported the Democratic Party.

26. Temple, *East Tennessee and the Civil War*, 179–223, 340–55; *Proceedings of the E.T. Convention*, 19–28; Patton, *Unionism and Reconstruction in Tennessee*, 10–25; Lacy, *Vanquished Volunteers*, 168–82.
27. Jesse Burt, "East Tennessee, Lincoln, and Sherman, pt. 1," East Tennessee Historical Society *Publications* 34 (1962): 3–5; James W. McKee Jr., "Felix K. Zollicoffer: Confederate Defender of East Tennessee," East Tennessee Historical Society *Publications* 43 (1971): 35, 43–44.
28. Scott and Angel, *History of the Thirteenth Regiment*, 274.
29. McKee, "Felix K. Zollicoffer," 36, 37.
30. Ibid., 40; *OR* I, 4, 374.
31. *Knoxville Whig*, August 10, 1861.
32. *OR* I, 4, 393.
33. Ibid., 4, 379.
34. *OR* II, 1, 837–38.
35. Temple, *East Tennessee and the Civil War*, 370–71. Apparently there was a discrepancy as to how much money W.B. Carter received from the Federal government. Oliver Temple reported that Carter told him he received only $2,500. However, Andrew Johnson wrote a letter to the president in November 1862 claiming that Carter had received $20,000 from the Federal government, of which $9,000 was unaccounted.
36. *OR* II, 1, 890; Scott and Angel, *History of the Thirteenth Regiment*, 59–63.
37. William B. Carter to Oliver P. Temple, April 11, 1895, O.P. Temple Papers, University of Tennessee Special Collections.
38. Among the men assisting Stover were: John G. Burchfield, John Burrows, Lafayette Cameron, J.D. Carriger, Landon Carter, Gilson O. Collins, Watson Collins, James T. Davenport, Samuel Davenport, Daniel Ellis, John Fondrin, Henderson Garland, William Gourley, Jacob Hendrickson, Mark Hendrickson, W.F.M. Hyder, Jonas H. Keen, George Maston, George Moody, B.M.G. O'Brien, Berry Pritchard, James P. Scott, Henry Slagle, Thomas Tipton, Benjamin F. Treadway, James Williams and Pleasant M. Williams.
39. Scott and Angel, *History of the Thirteenth Regiment*, 66–67.
40. Ibid., 67; Abraham Jobe, *Autobiography*, Archives of Appalachia, East Tennessee State University, Johnson City, TN, Box 1, 117.
41. Daniel Ellis, *Thrilling Adventures of Daniel Ellis* (1867; repr., Johnson City, 1989), 28; Scott and Angel, *History of the Thirteenth Regiment*, 69–75, 390. In addition to the Holston River Bridge in Sullivan County, the Hiwassee River Bridge in Bradley County, the Lick Creek Bridge in Greene County and two bridges over Chickamauga Creek near Chattanooga were also destroyed. For various complications due to enemy guards and poor planning, the remaining four bridges remained operational to the Confederacy.
42. *OR* I, 4, 231–32.
43. Ibid., 4, 347.
44. *OR* II, I, 843; Scott and Angel, *History of the Thirteenth Regiment*, 81.
45. *OR* I, 4, 321, 343.
46. Ibid., 342.

47. Ibid., 7, 480.
48. Ibid., 4, 359–60.
49. Ibid., 7, 530–31, 548–49, 926–28.
50. *OR* II, 1, 841.
51. Ibid., 1, 848.
52. *OR* I, 52 (2), 207.
53. *OR* II, 1, 851.
54. Temple, *East Tennessee and the Civil War*, 393–98; *OR* II, 1, 849; *OR* I, 7, 747–48; Fisher, *War at Every Door*, 58; W.G. Brownlow, *Sketches of the Rise, Progress, and Decline of Secession* (Philadelphia: George W. Childs, 1862), 311, 420–21.
55. *OR* II, 1, 848.
56. Ibid., 1, 846–47.
57. Scott and Angel, *History of the Thirteenth Regiment*, 76, 288.
58. "From Leonidas C. Houk," December 7, 1861, in *The Papers of Andrew Johnson*, eds. Leroy P. Graf and Ralph W. Haskins (Knoxville, TN, 1979), 5: 40–41.
59. William H. Barnes, *The Fortieth Congress of the United States: Historical and Biographical*, vol. 2 (New York: George E. Perine, 1870), 251.
60. Deposition of James Meeks, December 20, 1867, in *Papers in the Case of J. Powell v. R.R. Butler*, 7.
61. Kermit L. Hall, "West H. Humphreys and the Crisis of the Union," *Tennessee Historical Quarterly* 34 (1975): 55, 56; Depositions of Alfred T. Gourley, Hamilton C. Smith, David A. Taylor, December 12, 1867, in *Papers in the Case of J. Powell v. R.R. Butler*, 53–58.
62. Scott and Angel, *History of the Thirteenth Regiment*, 95.
63. Jobe, *Autobiography*, 118; Scott and Angel, *History of the Thirteenth Regiment*, 96.
64. *OR* II, 1, 853.
65. Ellis, *Adventures of Daniel Ellis*, 41, 44, 236; Fisher, *War at Every Door*, 62–65; Temple, *East Tennessee and the Civil War*, 426; Scott and Angel, *History of the Thirteenth Regiment*, 95, 136, 141, 148.
66. Ellis, *Adventures of Daniel Ellis*, 261, 321, 328, 337; Scott and Angel, *History of the Thirteenth Regiment*, 318, 324, 327, 338, 361. While Ellis, Scott and Angel refer to these men with rank identifications such as captain or colonel, Confederate military records are sketchy and it is unclear as to what regiments, if any, they belonged. It is quite possible they were leaders of irregular groups. This author has chosen the rank based on the sources indicated.
67. Scott and Angel, *History of the Thirteenth Regiment*, 339–40; Ellis, *Adventures of Daniel Ellis*, 329–31.
68. "From Robert L. Stanford," *Johnson Papers*, December 3, 1861, in *The Papers of Andrew Johnson*, eds. Leroy P. Graf and Ralph W. Haskins (Knoxville, TN, 1979), 5: 86–87.
69. Statement of Roderick R. Butler, April 8, 1868, in *Testimony in the Case of Hon. R.R. Butler*, 40th Cong., 2nd sess., S. Misc. Doc. 82, 1. Daniel Ellis wrote in his autobiography that Jones made his escape from prison by joining the Confederate army, but there are no records that indicate this was the case.
70. Ellis, *Adventures of Daniel Ellis*, 258–63.

71. Scott and Angel, *History of the Thirteenth Regiment*, 329; Ellis, *Adventures of Daniel Ellis*, 290–91, 299.
72. Ellis, *Adventures of Daniel Ellis*, 291–95, 300–5.
73. Scott and Angel, *History of the Thirteenth Regiment*, 322–27.
74. "From Horace Maynard," April 29, 1862, in *The Papers of Andrew Johnson*, 5: 348.
75. "To Edwin M. Stanton," June 21, 1862, in *The Papers of Andrew Johnson*, 5: 495–96.
76. "Horace Maynard to Abraham Lincoln," October 14, 1862, Roy P. Basler, ed., *The Collected Works of Abraham Lincoln* (New Brunswick, NJ, 1953–55), 6: 373.
77. Depositions of Daniel Ellis, Christopher C. Wilcox and John K. Miller, December 12, 1867, in *Papers in the Case of J. Powell v. R.R. Butler*, 53, 55, 59.
78. Deposition of Richard H. Butler, December 24, 1867, in *Papers in the Case of J. Powell v. R.R. Butler*, 47–48.
79. "Speech to Davidson County Citizens," March 22, 1862, in *The Papers of Andrew Johnson*, 5: 235.
80. Clifton Hall, *Andrew Johnson: Military Governor* (Princeton, NJ, 1916), 176–80; Scott and Angel, *History of the Thirteenth Regiment*, 112.

Chapter 2

81. Thomas L. Connelly, *Civil War Tennessee: Battles and Leaders* (Knoxville: University of Tennessee Press, 1979), 24–32.
82. *OR* I, 10 (2), 56–58; Hall, *Andrew Johnson*, 42.
83. Hall, *Andrew Johnson*, 51.
84. *OR* I, 10 (2), 126, 128–29, 180; *OR* I, 16 (2), 121–22.
85. "To Edwin M. Stanton," May 11, 1862, in *The Papers of Andrew Johnson*, 5: 378n; James A. Ramage, *Rebel Raiders: The Life of General John Hunt Morgan* (Lexington, KY, 1986), 228.
86. *OR* I, 16 (2), 118–19, 159; "Lincoln to Johnson," July 3, 1862, in *The Collected Works of Lincoln*, 5: 302–3.
87. "Authorization to Raise Troops," March 28, 1863, in *The Papers of Andrew Johnson*, 6: 198–99.
88. Scott and Angel, *History of the Thirteenth Regiment*, 110.
89. *OR* I, 30 (3), 660.
90. Originally designated the Twelfth Tennessee Volunteer Cavalry, Governor Andrew Johnson ordered the number changed from Twelfth to Thirteenth Tennessee Cavalry on December 31, 1863.
91. Civil War Centennial Commission, *Tennesseans in the Civil War: A Military History of Confederate and Union Units*, part I (Nashville, TN, 1964), 351; Scott and Angel, *History of the Thirteenth Regiment*, 120–23.
92. Daniel S. Head, Civil War Pension Complete File, certificate number 109478, National Archives and Records Administration, Washington, D.C.; Daniel S. Head, Compiled Service Records of Union Soldiers Who Served in Organizations from the State of Tennessee, Record Group 94, National Archives and Records Administration, Washington, D.C.

93. Civil War Centennial Commission, *Tennesseans in the Civil War*, 351; Scott and Angel, *History of the Thirteenth Regiment*, 120–23.
94. Scott and Angel, *History of the Thirteenth Regiment*, 124–28; *OR* I, 31 (1), 276.
95. Officially, the guard was attached to Gillem's Fourth Division of the Department of the Cumberland. Colonel Miller was placed in charge of the Third Brigade of the governor's guard, which consisted of the Eighth, Ninth and Thirteenth Tennessee Cavalry Regiments.
96. George Frederick Root composed the "Battle Cry of Freedom" in 1862.
97. Scott and Angel, *History of the Thirteenth Regiment*, 130–33.
98. Ibid., 133–34.
99. "George M. Dugger to William H. Dugger," March 20, 1864. Original letter is in the possession of a Dugger ancestor, Bill Ward of Columbus, Kansas.
100. Scott and Angel, *History of the Thirteenth Regiment*, 136–37.
101. "George M. Dugger to William H. Dugger," March 20, 1864.
102. Scott and Angel, *History of the Thirteenth Regiment*, 138.
103. *Louisville Daily Journal*, April 28, 1864; Walter T. Durham, *Rebellion Revisited: A History of Sumner County, Tennessee from 1861 to 1870* (Gallatin, TN: Sumner County Museum Association, 1982), 194.
104. Scott and Angel, *History of the Thirteenth Regiment*, 145–47.
105. Ibid., 141.
106. Ibid., 140–41.
107. Alice Williamson Diary, Flowers Collection, Special Collections Library, Online Archival Collection, library.duke.edu/rubenstein/scriptorium/williamson, Duke University, Durham, North Carolina. According to Walter T. Durham in *Rebellion Revisited*, Alice Williamson was seventeen years old in 1864, and she kept a diary from February to September 1864 while living in Gallatin, Tennessee.
108. Guy Vernor Henry, *Military Record of Civilian Appointments in the United States Army* (New York: D. Van Nostrand Publisher, 1873), 113–14.
109. *OR* I, 32 (1), 259.
110. Ibid., 23 (1), 231.
111. William H. Ingerton, Civil War Pension Complete File, certificate number 63024, National Archives and Records Administration, Washington, D.C.
112. Scott and Angel, *History of the Thirteenth Regiment*, 142–44.
113. Ibid.,149.
114. "From John K. Miller," July 31, 1864, in *The Papers of Andrew Johnson*, 7: 161–62.
115. "From William H. Robinson," June 11, 1864, in *The Papers of Andrew Johnson*, 6: 733.
116. "From James B. Wyatt," June 17, 1864, in *The Papers of Andrew Johnson*, 6: 742–43.
117. Scott and Angel, *History of the Thirteenth Regiment*, 150.
118. *OR* I, 39 (2), 75–76.
119. "From Roderick R. Butler," July 5, 1864, in *The Papers of Andrew Johnson*, 7: 12–13; "From East Tennessee Unionists," July 27, 1864, in *The Papers of Andrew Johnson*, 7: 52–53.
120. *OR* I, 39 (2), 80.
121. "Speech near Gallatin," July 19, 1864, in *The Papers of Andrew Johnson*, 7: 70.
122. *OR* I, 34, 486; Scott and Angel, *History of the Thirteenth Regiment*, 160, 315.

Chapter 3

123. Ramage, *Rebel Raider*, 197, 237.
124. "Order re Governor's Guard," August 1, 1864, in *The Papers of Andrew Johnson*, 7:70.
125. Ramage, *Rebel Raider*, 218, 226–30.
126. Baggett, *Homegrown Yankees*, 324; Scott and Angel, *History of the Thirteenth Regiment*, 158; William G. Brownlow to Johnson, August 18, 1864, in *The Papers of Andrew Johnson*, 7: 100–1.
127. Baggett, *Homegrown Yankees*, 324; Scott and Angel, *History of the Thirteenth Regiment*, 158.
128. Scott and Angel, *History of the Thirteenth Regiment*, 159–60; OR I, 39 (1), 488–89.
129. *Greeneville Democrat*, "General Morgan's Death," November 4, 1899; S.H. Arnell, "Unwritten History: The Midnight Ride," *National Tribune*, October 20, 1892; P.W. Horn, "Death of John Hunt Morgan: A Greenvillian Gives His Version of the Affair," *The Bee* (Earlington, KY), April 18, 1895.
130. Based on the 1860 census, Jimmy Leedy would have been around thirteen or fourteen at this time. The last name is sometimes spelled Leady, Leidy or Leahy.
131. James M. Fry, *The Death of General John H. Morgan and What Led Up to It: By an East Tennessee Confederate Scout* (Wills Point, TX, n.d.), 7; Horn, "Death of John Hunt Morgan."
132. Arnell, "Unwritten History"; Ramage, *Rebel Raiders*, 233.
133. Scott and Angel, *History of the Thirteenth Regiment*, 166; Ramage, *Rebel Raiders*, 234; Richard H. Doughty, *Greeneville: One Hundred Year Portrait, Greeneville, TN, 1975* (Greeneville, TN, 1975), 31.
134. Brownlow as quoted in Arnell, "Unwritten History"; Doughty, *Greeneville*, 232; Scott and Angel, *History of the Thirteenth Regiment*, 166–67; *OR* I, 39 (1), 488–90.
135. Scott and Angel, *History of the Thirteenth Regiment*, 169. An exhibit at the Nathanael Greene museum in Greeneville speculates that the citizen bearing the warning to Ingerton may have been Edmund B. Miller. Although Morgan only had about half as many troops as reported by this individual, Ingerton was a regular army man and was never known to shy away from a fight. He saw a great opportunity to capture a high-profile Confederate officer.
136. Arnell, "Unwritten History."
137. Ramage, *Rebel Raider*, 236.
138. *OR* I, 39 (1), 491, 492.
139. Private Andrew Campbell was a native of Dublin, Ireland, and had arrived in the United States shortly before the war. He was drafted into the Second Arkansas Infantry, CSA, but deserted early in 1864 to join the Thirteenth Tennessee. See Ed Speer, "One Moment of Glory: The Life of Private Andrew Campbell of the Thirteenth Tennessee Cavalry, U.S.A.," *Tennessee Historical Quarterly* 60 (2001): 284–93.
140. Scott and Angel, *History of the Thirteenth Regiment*, 175.
141. John B. Brownlow to Oliver P. Temple, September 7, 1864, O.P. Temple Papers; Scott and Angel, *History of the Thirteenth Regiment*, 175–76; Arnell, "Unwritten History."

142. Arnell, "Unwritten History"; Ramage, *Rebel Raider*, 238–39; Scott and Angel, *History of the Thirteenth Regiment*, 176.
143. Andrew Campbell as quoted in Ramage, *Rebel Raiders*, 237–38.
144. Scott and Angel, *History of the Thirteenth Regiment*, 176–77; *OR* I, 39 (1), 489–90.
145. Arnell, "Unwritten History"; Ramage, *Rebel Raider*, 238–39; Scott and Angel, *History of the Thirteenth Regiment*, 177; Forrest Conklin, "Footnotes on the Death of John Hunt Morgan," *Tennessee Historical Quarterly* 34 (1976): 386; *OR* I, 38 (5), 812.
146. Scott and Angel, *History of the Thirteenth Regiment*, 184–85; "To Abraham Lincoln," in *The Papers of Andrew Johnson*, 7: 157.
147. *Knoxville Whig*, "Death of Morgan," September 4, 1864.
148. *Richmond Whig*, September 6, 1864.
149. Quoted in Ramage, *Rebel Raider*, 243.
150. *Richmond Daily Dispatch*, "The Death of General Morgan," September 10, 1864.
151. *Richmond Whig*, September 13, 1864; Ramage, *Rebel Raider*, 239–44; Howard Swiggett, *The Rebel Raider: A Life of John Hunt Morgan* (Indianapolis, 1934), 284–95. After the war, Sarah Thompson, a Greeneville Unionist, claimed that she had informed Gillem. Her husband served as a Union courier and was captured and executed as a spy by some of Morgan's men. After the war, President Andrew Johnson gave a deposition supporting her claims.
152. C.A. Withers, "Who Betrayed General Morgan? An Account of His Treacherous Surprise and Brutal Murder," *Savannah Morning News*, October 25, 1871.
153. W.A. Smith and Wallace Milam, eds., "The Death of John Hunt Morgan: A Memoir of James M. Fry," *Tennessee Historical Quarterly* 19 (1960): 60–63; Fry, "Death of Morgan," 10–11.
154. Conklin, "Footnotes on the Death of Morgan," 384; Doughty, *Greeneville*, 227–28.
155. Doughty, *Greeneville*, 227–28; Withers, "Who Betrayed General Morgan?"
156. Horn, "Death of John Morgan."
157. *OR* I, 39 (1), 491–92; Ramage, *Rebel Raider*, 241.

Chapter 4

158. Robert B. McCall, Civil War Pension Complete File, certificate number 105554, National Archives and Records Administration, Washington, D.C.; Scott and Angel, *History of the Thirteenth Regiment*, 153–54.
159. Scott and Angel, *History of the Thirteenth Regiment*, 190–92.
160. Ibid., 195–97.
161. Ibid., 198–200; *OR* I, 39 (1), 845–846.
162. Scott and Angel, *History of the Thirteenth Regiment*, 201.
163. *OR* I, 39 (1), 851.
164. Larry Gordon, *The Last Confederate General: John C. Vaughn and His East Tennessee Cavalry* (Minneapolis, MN: Zenith Press, 2009), 129–31; Scott and Angel, *History of the Thirteenth Regiment*, 202; *OR* I, 39 (1), 892.
165. Scott and Angel, *History of the Thirteenth Regiment*, 204; *OR* I, 39 (1), 886, 888–89.

166. Scott and Angel, *History of the Thirteenth Regiment*, 207.
167. *OR* I, 39 (1), 889.
168. Ibid., 39 (1), 893.
169. Ibid., 39 (1), 885–86.
170. Ibid.; Scott and Angel, *History of the Thirteenth Regiment*, 210–11.
171. *OR* I, 39 (1), 886.
172. John B. Brownlow to Oliver P. Temple, April 7, 1895, O.P. Temple Papers.
173. *OR* I, 39 (1), 886–87.
174. Ibid., 39 (1), 893, 897–98.
175. John B. Brownlow to Oliver P. Temple, April 7, 1895, O.P. Temple Papers.
176. Scott and Angel, *History of the Thirteenth Regiment*, 210–14.
177. James I. Robertson Jr., "Houses of Horror: Danville's Civil War Prisons," *Virginia Magazine of History and Biography* 69 (July 1961): 329; *OR* II, 6, 438–39.
178. Robertson, "Houses of Horror," 330–31; Homer Baxter Sprague, *Lights and Shadows in a Confederate Prison: A Personal Experience, 1864–1865* (New York, 1915), 79–80.
179. Due to the lack of accurate recordkeeping, it is difficult to know exactly how many men from the regiment were confined at Danville. According to service records, at least one hundred men were classified as prisoners of war and over twenty reported to have died prisoners of war.
180. Robertson, "Houses of Horror," 340; *OR* II, 7, 870–71.
181. George H. Putnam, *A Prisoner of War in Virginia, 1864–1865* (New York, 1912), 40.
182. Ibid., 36, 40–41, 43; Sprague, *Lights and Shadows in a Confederate Prison*, 79–80; Alfred S. Roe, *In a Rebel Prison* (Providence, RI, 1891), 12.
183. Robertson, "Houses of Horror," 337.
184. Putnam, *A Prisoner of War in Virginia*, 36; Roe, *In a Rebel Prison*, 15.
185. Solon Hyde, *A Captive of War* (New York, 1925), 108–9; Asa B. Isham, *Prisoners of War and Military Prisons* (Cincinnati, OH, 1890), 202–3.
186. Robertson, "Houses of Horror," 333. At least three soldiers of the Thirteenth Tennessee are buried at the Danville National Cemetery: Ephraim Gentry, Samuel Kehill and Calvin Whaley.
187. *Mountain City, Tennessee Tomahawk*, "Vada Payne Curd Has Letter Her Grandfather Wrote During the Civil War," n.d. From the Original Johnson County Tennessee Genealogy Page jctcuzins.org/letters/letter11.html (accessed July 31, 2013).
188. *OR* I, 38(5), 409–10, 940.
189. Joshua H. Walker, Civil War Union Court-Martial Records, March 9, 1864, Records of the Judge Advocate General, Record Group 153, National Archives, Washington, D.C.
190. Scott and Angel, *History of the Thirteenth Regiment*, 215–16.
191. U.S. Bureau of the Census, 1860, Ripley, Brown, B.P. Stacey, 226.
192. Scott and Angel, *History of the Thirteenth Regiment*, 269–70.
193. Ibid., 217–18.

Chapter 5

194. John L. Hyder, Compiled Service Records of Union Soldiers Who Served in Organizations from the State of Tennessee, Record Group 94, National Archives and Records Administration, Washington, D.C.
195. *OR* I, 45 (1), 1073–74; Robert C. Whisonant, "Geology and the Civil War in Southwestern Virginia: The Wythe County Lead Mines," *Virginia Minerals* 42 (May 1996): 17.
196. *OR* I, 45 (1), 1073–74.
197. Ibid., 45 (2), 54, 402.
198. Baggett, *Homegrown Yankees*, 335.
199. Scott and Angel, *History of the Thirteenth Regiment*, 220–21.
200. Ibid., 221.
201. Ibid., 222.
202. Ibid., 222–23.
203. Ibid., 223.
204. Whisonant, "The Wythe County Lead Mines," 17; Scott and Angel, *History of the Thirteenth Regiment*, 223-24.
205. Whisonant, "The Wythe County Lead Mines," 15.
206. Scott and Angel, *History of the Thirteenth Regiment*, 225.
207. *OR* I, 45 (1), 812.
208. Ibid.
209. Ibid., 813.
210. Ibid.
211. Scott and Angel, *History of the Thirteenth Regiment*, 229.
212. Whisonant, "The Wythe County Lead Mines," 17–18; *OR* I, 45 (2), 402.
213. *OR* I, 49 (1), 616–17.
214. Ibid., 49 (1), 663.
215. Ina Woestermeyer Van Noppen, *Stoneman's Last Raid* (Raleigh, NC, 1961), x–xi.
216. William R. Trotter, *Bushwhackers!: The Civil War in the Mountains* (Winston-Salem, NC, 1991), 251.
217. *OR* I, 49 (2), 12–13.
218. Weand, "Our Last Campaign and Pursuit of Jeff Davis," 493.
219. Ibid.
220. James C.J. Lewis, Civil War Pension Complete File, certificate number 1123841, National Archives and Records Administration, Washington, D.C.; Andrew Greer, Civil War Pension Complete File, certificate number 913480, National Archives and Records Administration, Washington, D.C.; Joel Greer, Civil War Pension Complete File, certificate number 140941, National Archives and Records Administration, Washington, D.C.
221. Van Noppen, *Stoneman's Last Raid*, 15–16.
222. *OR* I, 49 (2), 112.
223. Van Noppen, *Stoneman's Last Raid*, 18, 25; *OR* I, 49 (1), 331.
224. Howard A. Buzby, "With Gillem's Tennesseans on the Yadkin," in Charles H. Kirk's *History of the Fifteenth Pennsylvania Volunteer Cavalry*, 523–24.

225. Van Noppen, *Stoneman's Last Raid*, 33; *OR* I, 49 (1), 331–32; Scott and Angel, *History of the Thirteenth Regiment*, 235.
226. Chris J. Hartley, *Stoneman's Raid: 1865* (Winston-Salem, NC: John F. Blair Publisher, 2010), 138–42; William Jenkins, Compiled Service Records of Union Soldiers Who Served in Organizations from the State of Tennessee, Record Group 94, National Archives and Records Administration, Washington, D.C.; *OR* I, 49 (1), 332; Scott and Angel, *History of the Thirteenth Regiment*, 236.
227. Van Noppen, *Stoneman's Last Raid*, 37–38; *OR* I, 49 (1), 332–33.
228. Cornelia Phillips Spencer, *The Last Ninety Days of the War in North Carolina* (New York, 1866), 199; Hartley, *Stoneman's Raid*, 230.
229. *OR* I, 49 (1), 333; Scott and Angel, *History of the Thirteenth Regiment*, 238; Spencer, *Last Ninety Days*, 200; Van Noppen, *Stoneman's Last Raid*, 63; Weand, "Our Last Campaign and Pursuit of Jeff Davis," 504.
230. Hartley, *Stoneman's Raid*, 247–48.
231. Ibid., 248–49.
232. Spencer, *Last Ninety Days*, 201; Hartley, *Stoneman's Raid*, 249–50.
233. Spencer, *Last Ninety Days*, 201–2; Hartley, *Stoneman's Raid*, 250.
234. Hartley, *Stoneman's Raid*, 251–52.
235. *OR* I, 49 (1), 334; Spencer, *Last Ninety Days*, 205.
236. Van Noppen, *Stoneman's Last Raid*, 56–57, 67.
237. *OR* I, 49 (1), 334–36; Van Noppen, *Stoneman's Last Raid*, 69.
238. *OR* I, 49 (1), 324–25.
239. Spencer, *Last Ninety Days*, 216–17.
240. Hartley, *Stoneman's Raid*, 295–96; Spencer, *Last Ninety Days*, 218.
241. Hartley, *Stoneman's Raid*, 296–97.
242. Spencer, *Last Ninety Days*, 218.
243. Ibid., 219.
244. Ibid., 220–22.
245. John Inscoe and Gordon B. McKinney, *The Heart of Confederate Appalachia: Western North Carolina in the Civil War* (Chapel Hill: University of North Carolina Press, 2000), 258–59.
246. Scott and Angel, *History of the Thirteenth Regiment*, 240.
247. Inscoe and McKinney, *The Heart of Confederate Appalachia*, 262.
248. Mary Brown as quoted in Inscoe and McKinney, *The Heart of Confederate Appalachia*, 263.
249. *OR* I, 49 (1), 335–36.
250. Ibid., 49 (2), 457.
251. Ibid., 49 (1), 546.
252. Catherine Polk as quoted in Inscoe and McKinney, *The Heart of Confederate Appalachia*, 264.
253. James Martin as quoted in Trotter, *Bushwhackers*, 286.
254. Spencer, *Last Ninety Days*, 232–33; Van Noppen, *Stoneman's Last Raid*, 79, 90.
255. Ellis, *Adventures of Daniel Ellis*, 233; Scott and Angel, *History of the Thirteenth Regiment*, 359–60.
256. *OR* I, 49 (1), 546–47.

Chapter 6

257. Baggett, *Homegrown Yankees*, 358.
258. Scott and Angel, *History of the Thirteenth Regiment*, 242.
259. *OR* I, 49 (1), 549–50.
260. Alexander H. Stephens, *Recollections of Alexander H. Stephens: His Diary Kept with a Prisoner at Fort Warren, Boston Harbor* (New York, 1910), 143–44; Scott and Angel, *History of the Thirteenth Regiment*, 242–44; *OR* I, 49 (1), 552.
261. Scott and Angel, *History of the Thirteenth Regiment*, 246–47.
262. Ibid., 247–48.
263. Ibid., 249–50, 252–55.
264. John K. Miller, Compiled Service Records of Union Soldiers Who Served in Organizations from the State of Tennessee, Record Group 94, National Archives and Records Administration, Washington, D.C.
265. John K. Miller, Civil War Union Court-Martial Records, October 16, 1865, Records of the Judge Advocate General, Record Group 153, National Archives, Washington, D.C.
266. Ibid.
267. Ibid.
268. Ibid.
269. Asa Reece, "Case Files of Applications from Former Confederates for Presidential Pardons ('Amnesty Papers'), 1865–1867," Record Group 94, Records of the Adjutant General's Office, 1780–1917, National Archives and Records Administration, Washington, D.C.
270. Madison T. Peoples, "Case Files of Applications from Former Confederates for Presidential Pardons ('Amnesty Papers'), 1865–1867," Record Group 94, Records of the Adjutant General's Office, 1780–1917, National Archives and Records Administration, Washington, D.C.
271. Daniel Ellis, *Thrilling Adventures*, 328; Peoples Application.
272. Isaac E. Wilson, "Case Files of Applications from Former Confederates for Presidential Pardons ('Amnesty Papers'), 1865–1867," Record Group 94, Records of the Adjutant General's Office, 1780–1917, National Archives and Records Administration, Washington, D.C.
273. George Shults, "Case Files of Applications from Former Confederates for Presidential Pardons ('Amnesty Papers'), 1865–1867," Record Group 94, Records of the Adjutant General's Office, 1780–1917, National Archives and Records Administration, Washington, D.C.
274. Isaac P. Tipton, "Case Files of Applications from Former Confederates for Presidential Pardons ('Amnesty Papers'), 1865–1867," Record Group 94, Records of the Adjutant General's Office, 1780–1917, National Archives and Records Administration, Washington, D.C. Tipton had two sons serve in the Confederate army; neither survived. George Heatherly killed Robert Tipton, and Eldridge Tipton died of pneumonia during the last year of the war.
275. George D. Taylor, Henry H. Taylor and Nat M. Taylor, "Case Files of Applications from Former Confederates for Presidential Pardons ('Amnesty Papers'), 1865–1867," Record Group 94, Records of the Adjutant General's

Office, 1780–1917, National Archives and Records Administration, Washington, D.C.
276. H.M. Folsom, "Case Files of Applications from Former Confederates for Presidential Pardons ('Amnesty Papers'), 1865–1867," Record Group 94, Records of the Adjutant General's Office, 1780–1917, National Archives and Records Administration, Washington, D.C.
277. George W. Vaught, Civil War Pension Complete File, certificate number 109102, National Archives and Records Administration, Washington, D.C.
278. Oliver Wendell Holmes, address to John Sedgwick Post No. 4, Grand Army of the Republic, May 30, 1884, Keene, NH; David W. Blight, *Race and Reunion: The Civil War in American Memory* (Cambridge, MA, 2001), 96.

CHAPTER 7

279. *New York Times*, "In the Name of Andrew Jackson," October 10, 1896; *Elizabethton Mountaineer*, "McKinley's Speech to the East Tennessee Delegation," October 10, 1896.
280. *Elizabethton Mountaineer*, "The Re-Union at Butler," October 16, 1896; Scott and Angel, *History of the Thirteenth Regiment*, 449.
281. Scott and Angel, *History of the Thirteenth Regiment*, 366–67.
282. Ibid., 289.
283. *Elizabethton Mountaineer*, "The Re-Union at Butler," October 16, 1896.
284. Scott and Angel, *History of the Thirteenth Regiment*, 178.
285. Christopher C. Wilcox, letter to the editor, *Jonesboro Union Flag*, May 5, 1866.
286. *Little Rock Morning Republican*, "General John H. Morgan: How He Was Killed," September 14, 1871.
287. J.W. Scully, "General John Morgan," *Richmond Times-Dispatch*, July 17, 1903.
288. Scott and Angel, *History of the Thirteenth Regiment*, 181–83.
289. Ibid., 256; John M. Wilcox, "General Morgan's Death," *Greeneville Democrat*, November 16, 1899.
290. Susan Pendleton Lee, *Lee's Advanced School History of the United States* (Richmond, VA, 1895), 509–10.
291. Wilcox, "General Morgan's Death."
292. A.B. Wilson, "Death of Morgan: Correction of Errors in Some Alleged Histories," *National Tribune*, January 24, 1902.
293. *Greeneville New Era*, "Colonel John K. Miller," July 8, 1903.
294. Robert M. McBride and Dan Robinson, *Biographical Directory of the Tennessee General Assembly v. II 1861–1901* (Nashville, TN, 1979), 622–23.
295. *Johnson City Comet*, "Col. John K. Miller Dead," July 16, 1903.
296. Scott and Angel, *History of the Thirteenth Regiment*, 266–67.
297. Ingerton pension file; Scott and Angel, *History of the Thirteenth Regiment*, 215–16; Richard B. McCaslin, *Portraits of Conflict: A Photographic History of Tennessee in the Civil War* (Fayetteville, AR, 2007), 226.
298. U.S. Bureau of the Census, 1860, Walla Walla District, Washington Territory, Anna V. Mayo, 300; Ingerton pension file.

299. Guy Vernor Henry, *Military Record of Civilian Appointments in the United States Army*, vol. 2 (New York: D. Van Nostrand Publisher, 1873), 113–14; Francis White Johnson, *A History of Texas and Texans*, vol. 4 (Chicago: American Historical Society, 1914), 2047.
300. "Pennsylvania, Philadelphia City Death Certificates, 1803–1915," index. FamilySearch, Salt Lake City, Utah, 2008, 2010. From originals housed at the Philadelphia City Archives. "Death Records."
301. Ingerton pension file.
302. Ibid.
303. *Urbana Union*, August 4, 1864; "Ohio, County Marriages, 1789–1994," index and images, FamilySearch (familysearch.org/pal:/MM9.1.1/XZK4-39N: accessed July 20, 2013), William H. Ingerton and Martha H. Sargent, 1864.
304. Scott and Angel, *History of the Thirteenth Regiment*, 156.
305. Letter from Ada Thornburg to Carrie Stakely, December 8, 1864, Hall-Stakely Papers, McClung Collection, Knox County Public Library, Tennessee.
306. Ingerton pension file; *Urban Union*, January 11, 1865; Johnson, *A History of Texas and Texans*, 2047.
307. Brazilliah P. Stacy, Civil War Pension Complete File, certificate number 822651, National Archives and Records Administration, Washington, D.C.; "Stacy & Angel" advertisement, *Jonesboro Union Flag*, April 8, 1879.
308. "Obituary," *Knoxville Daily Chronicle*, September 22, 1882.
309. Margaret Hyder DeVault Collection, Series I, Box 1, Folder 6, Archives of Appalachia, East Tennessee State University, Johnson City; Scott and Angel, *History of the Thirteenth Regiment*, 301.
310. Samuel W. Scott, Civil War Pension Complete File, certificate number 713015, National Archives and Records Administration, Washington, D.C; *Elizabethton Mountaineer*, "The History of the 13th Tennessee Cavalry," August 8, 1902.
311. Frank Merritt, *Later History of Carter County, 1865–1980* (Carter County, TN, 1986), 53.
312. *Johnson City Comet*, "Loyal Carter Builds Shaft to War Heroes," September 12, 1912; *Bristol Herald Courier*, "Reunion of Veterans Held at Elizabethton," October 12, 1913.
313. Anne Elizabeth Marshall, *Creating a Confederate Kentucky: The Lost Cause and Civil War Memory in a Border State* (Chapel Hill, NC, 2010), 171–73; Edison H. Thomas, *John Hunt Morgan and His Raiders* (Lexington, KY, 1975), xi.
314. Andrew Campbell, Civil War Pension Complete File, application number 614504, National Archives and Records Administration, Washington, D.C.; *Index to Death Records in the City of St. Louis, 1850–1902* (St. Louis, 1999), 30: 528.
315. Merritt, *Later History of Carter County*, 61.
316. Ecclesiasticus 44:1, 7–9, 13. This is a book of the Apocrypha included by some churches in the Bible; it should not be confused with Ecclesiastes.

Index

A

Allen, James R. 8
Ammen, Jacob 72, 73, 75
Angel, Samuel 74, 128
  and Alexander Stephens 106
  friendship with B.P. Stacy 128
  regimental history 8, 14, 119, 129
  views of slavery 54
Asheville, North Carolina 101, 102, 103, 104
  Daniel Ellis's remarks about 103

B

Baxter, John 18
Bell, Dr. David 39
Bell, James
  brother of Dr. David Bell 39
  death of 39
Bell, John 13
Benjamin, Judah P. 30
  ordered execution of bridge burners 33
Branner, John R.
  concerned about bridges 31
  president of ET&V Railroad 30
  reports to Judah P. Benjamin 31
  requested Confederate troops 31
Breckinridge, General John C. 73, 74, 75, 83, 85, 88
bridge burning 27, 30, 35, 36, 118
  execution for 33
Bristol, Tennessee 21, 25, 27, 30, 33
Bristol, Virginia 83, 85
Brooks, William
  conscription officer 41
  death 41, 42
  Fifty-ninth Tennessee Confederate infantry 41
  revenge for his murder 42, 114
  son of Rueben Brooks 41
Brownlow, John B.
  criticism of Gillem 65, 75
  death of Morgan 67
  lieutenant colonel 65, 66, 67, 68, 75
  son of "Parson" Brownlow 65, 75
Brownlow, William "Parson" 14, 33, 68, 73
Buell, Don Carlos 31, 32, 45, 46, 47
Bulls Gap, Tennessee 62, 64, 71, 72, 73, 74, 75, 80, 83, 85, 114

INDEX

Burbridge, Stephen 85, 88
Burchfield, John G. 17, 18, 27, 121
  bridge burning 27
  circumstances surrounding John H.
    Morgan's death 122
  postwar life 129
Burton, Thomas 11
Butler, Anne Leitch
  mother of Roderick R. Butler 35
Butler, George
  father of Roderick R. Butler 35
Butler, Richard
  joined Confederate company 43
  son of Roderick R. Butler 43
Butler, Roderick R.
  and Confederate home guards 43
  and John K. Miller 43
  and Richard Butler 43
  arrested for treason 43
  as a judge 35
  call for volunteers 48
  commissioning a regiment 14, 43, 47
  death of 126
  defense of Unionists 35, 36, 126
  East Tennessee petition 59
  flag in honor of 126
  lieutenant colonel 48, 54
  postwar activities 114
  resignation of commission 54
  secessionists' opinion of 19, 23
  state representative 14, 19, 35, 36
  town named for 118
  veterans' reunions 126
Butler, Tennessee 8, 118, 129

C

Campbell, Andrew 121
  and John H. Morgan 66
  death of 132
  greeted with cheers 67
  postwar life 132
  promotion 67
  testifies about killing Morgan 66
  treatment of Morgan's body 66, 69, 122

Camp Dick Robinson 30, 37
Camp Gillem 51
Camp Nelson 48, 49, 50
Carter County, Tennessee 13, 17, 19,
  24, 39, 41, 43, 52, 100, 112,
  114, 122, 123
  arrests in 35, 36
  bridge burning 36
  conditions for Unionists 49
  Confederate sympathizers 34
  hardships 83
  rebellion 31
  split loyalties in 113
  Unionism 27, 34, 37, 39
  violence in 40, 41
Carter, James P.T. 24
Carter, Samuel P. 24, 32, 59, 82
  importance of East Tennessee
    invasion 32
  military aid to East Tennessee 59
Carter's Depot 25, 27, 31, 42, 72, 75
Carter, William B. 15, 19, 24
  bridge burning 32
  meeting with President Lincoln 24
Clay, Captain Henry B.
  identified John H. Morgan's body 66
  member of John H. Morgan's staff
    66
Cocke, William 18, 19
conscription 37, 40, 41, 42, 57, 91,
  113, 114
"contraband" 94, 98
  camps 53
  school burned 54
  soldiers' attitude toward 54
  soldiers terrorizing camps 15
Cunningham, Samuel A.
  son-in-law to Thomas A.R. Nelson
    26

D

Danville & Greensboro Railroad 94
Danville Prison 76, 77, 78, 79
Danville, Virginia 76, 78, 79, 97

INDEX

Davis, Jefferson 24, 30, 32, 36, 106
  and Patrick Dyer 108
  capture of 106
  conscription 37
  martial law in East Tennessee 33
  pardon of Harrison Self 34
  Union troops in pursuit of 104, 105, 106
disease 16, 52
  diarrhea 48, 79
  in prison camps 78, 79
  measles 52, 79
  smallpox 52, 79
  typhoid 79
Doughty, George W.
  and B.P. Stacy 81
  and Colonel Miller 82
  and Ellis Harper gang 53
  and William H. Ingerton 81
  appointed Gillem's chief of staff 82
  arrest 82
  passed over for promotion 55, 81
  promise to former Confederate troops 50
  recruiting 49
  supplies for Knoxville 50
Duvall, B.H. 39, 42, 114

E

East Tennessee and Georgia (ET&G) Railroad 21, 23
East Tennessee and Virginia (ET&V) Railroad 21, 23, 29
Echols, John 93
  commander of the District of Southwestern Virginia 69
  successor to John H. Morgan 69
Eighth Tennessee Union Cavalry 40, 72
Elizabethton Mountaineer
  publicized soldiers' reunion 118
Elizabethton, Tennessee 17, 18, 19, 25, 27, 42, 44, 72, 111, 129, 130
  encampment of Unionists 31
Ellis, Daniel 36, 37, 39, 40

  and Bill Waugh 40
  and Samuel McQueen 104
  and William Parker 40, 41
  clearing out home guard in East Tennessee 104
  commissioned a captain 103
  guide 43, 52
  killing William Parker 41
  remarks about Madison T. Peoples 112
Ellis, Mary
  appeal to General Stoneman 97
  witnessed Union soldiers in Salisbury, North Carolina 96
Emancipation Proclamation 15, 53
  news of 26
Emmert, George W. 26, 35

F

Folsom, Henderson M. 42, 114
  act of kindness toward Heatherly family 114
  petition for pardon 114
  Sixty-ninth North Carolina Confederate regiment "Thomas's Legion" 114
Fort Breckinridge 88, 89
Fry, Henry
  execution as bridge burner 33

G

Gallatin, Tennessee 53, 56, 59, 127
Gillem, Alvan C. 60, 61, 62, 64, 67, 71, 72, 73, 80, 83, 87, 88, 102
  and Asheville, North Carolina 102, 103
  and Bulls Gap 62, 73, 74
  and "contraband" 53
  and cossacks 90
  and death of John H. Morgan 67, 68, 69
  and "governor's guard" 74
  and Jimmy Leedy 64
  and Major Doughty 82

151

Index

and plundering of homes 100, 101
and Stoneman's raid 92, 95, 98, 100, 101, 102
and the death of John H. Morgan 121
and William H. Ingerton's death 81
attack at Greeneville 65
battle report of Salisbury, North Carolina 98
brigade improving 62
cavalry command 90
complaints about lack of reinforcements 74
complaints about lack of resources 74
criticism of 75
defensive position 75
denied report of killing prisoners 100
departure from Stoneman's raid 103
distaste for Lenoir, North Carolina 100
doubts about Greeneville march 65
druken troops 93
feud with Ammen 75
flag of truce 102
harsh treatment of civilians 100, 101
identified Jimmy Leedy as informant 121
investigates death of John H. Morgan 69
ordered Patterson's factory burned 92
plundering of houses 100, 101
political career 102
praise for Colonel John K. Miller 110
promotion 68
report to Andrew Johnson on retreat 74
retreat from Bulls Gap 74
Sherman's comments 59
Gourley, Alfred 36
    arrested as bridge burner 36
Gourley, William 27, 87, 103
    bridge burning 27
    death of 86
"governor's guard" 47, 50, 59, 61, 75

Greeneville Convention 21, 24
Greeneville, Tennessee 33, 62, 64, 65, 68, 102, 121
Guy, Thomas 11

H

Harmon, Jacob
    executed as bridge burner 33
Harmon, Thomas
    executed as bridge burner 33
Harper, Ellis 53
Harris, Isham
    governor of Tennessee 17, 18, 19
    members of legislature must take oath to Confederacy 35
    report to Jefferson Davis on bridge burning 32
    response to President Lincoln's call for volunteers 18
    support of secession 20
    threat of Unionists 23
Haun, Alex C.
    executed as bridge burner 33
Haynes, Landon C. 18, 24
    warns about Unionists in East Tennessee 24
Head, Daniel S. 8, 48
Head, Mary Miller
    wife of Daniel S. Head 8
Heatherly gang
    wanted for murder 42
Heatherly, George 41, 42
    enlisted with Tenth Tennessee Union regiment 42
    killed Robert Tipton 41
    killed William Brooks 41
Heatherly, Godfrey 41
    enlisted with Thirteenth Tennessee Union Cavalry 42
Heatherly, Thomas 41
    father of George, Godfrey and Thomas Jr. 41
Heatherly, Thomas, Jr. 42
    killed in retaliation 42

Index

Heiskell, Joseph B. 18, 19, 62
Hendrix, Harrison 26
Hendrix, Solomon H. 26, 35
Hensie, Jacob M.
  execution as bridge burner 33
Holmes, Justice Oliver Wendell
  address to veterans 116
Holston River Bridge 26
  burning of 25, 27, 29
home guards 11, 15, 37, 39, 40, 41, 42, 43, 47, 49, 79, 91, 95, 101, 109, 112
home Yankees 11, 12, 100
Houk, Leonidas C.
  frustrations of East Tennesseans 35
  hardship faced by East Tennesseans 35
Humphreys, Judge West Hughes 36

I

Ingerton, Anna
  awarded widow's pension 128
  death of 128
  desperate situation 126
  disputed pension 128
  gives birth to a daughter 127
  marriage to William H. Ingerton 126
  stillborn baby 127
  wife of William H. Ingerton 55, 126, 127, 128
Ingerton, Mattie 127
  death of husband 128
  disputed pension 128
  marriage to William H. Ingerton 127
  postwar life 128
  pregnant with son 128
  wife of William H. Ingerton 81, 127
Ingerton, William H. 54, 55, 56, 57, 59, 62, 64, 65, 72, 75, 80, 81, 126, 127, 128
  and discipline 58
  and Joshua H. Walker 80, 81
  attack at Greeneville 65
  character of 57, 126
  death of 80, 128
  funeral services 128
  letter to wife Anna 55
  military background 16, 55, 126
  "Order of Congratulation" 67
  pension 128
  personal life 126, 127, 128
  personal loss 55
  son born to Mattie 128
  son of Lieutenant Colonel W.H. Ingerton 128
  warning from Greeneville, Tennessee citizen 65

J

Jenkins, Stanford
  bridge guard 27
  identified bridge burners to Confederate leaders 34
  released by bridge burners 29
Jenkins, William 94
Jobe, Dr. Abraham 27, 37, 42
  prisoner in home 36
Johnson, Andrew 14, 15, 18, 20, 25, 33, 35, 44
  amnesty 111
  and Alvan C. Gillem 47, 53, 61, 67, 73, 74, 75
  and Captain James B. Wyatt 57, 58
  and John Hunt Morgan 46, 61, 67
  East Tennessee petition 59
  feud with Don Carlos Buell 45, 46
  "governor's guard" 47, 50, 59, 61, 75
  Henry Halleck's opinion of 46
  military aid to East Tennessee 31, 32, 43, 44, 47, 59
  military governor of Tennessee 44, 45, 46, 47, 53, 57, 58, 59, 60, 61, 67, 68, 73, 74, 75
  pardon for Henderson M. Folsom 114
  permission to raise troops 47
  president 103, 111, 114
  restoration of Colonel John K. Miller 111

Index

speech at Gallatin, Tennessee 59
worry about defense of Nashville 46
Johnson County, Tennessee 19, 20, 22, 35, 39, 48, 104, 112, 113, 114
   conditions for Unionists 49
   Confederate sympathizers 19, 112, 114
   recruiting troops 22
   recruitment of troops 39
   split loyalties 113
   Unionism 20, 40
   violence in 40, 104
Jones, Lafayette 39, 40
   and Bill Waugh 40
   killing of Bill Waugh 40
Jones, William
   bridge guard 27
   escape of 27

K

Kitzmiller, David 19
   letter to Governor Harris 19
   opinion of Roderick R. Butler 19
   Unionists threatening secessionists 19
Knoxville Convention 20
Knoxville, Tennessee 23, 33, 43, 47, 60, 62, 72, 73, 75, 80, 83, 85, 88, 90, 98, 100, 109, 111, 126, 127, 128
   arrival of Union troops 47
   Burnside's army in 50
   siege of 50
   troops muster 48

L

Ledbetter, Danville 33, 37
   execution of bridge burners 33
   proclamation to citizens of East Tennessee 33
Lee, General Robert E. 98
   surrender 93, 102, 103
   transfer of prisoners from Richmond 76
Lee, Susan P.
   textbook controversy 122
Letcher, John
   governor of Virginia 29

Lick Creek Bridge
   burning of bridge 33
Limestone Cove tragedy 39
"Lincolnites" 23, 31, 39
Lincoln, President Abraham 19, 23, 25, 42, 44, 45, 46, 47
   and East Tennessee 32
   call for troops 23
   defense of Andrew Johnson 46
   Maynard pleads for aid in East Tennessee 43
   meeting with William B. Carter 25
   news of assassination 102
   recruitment of troops in East Tennessee 47
Louisville and Nashville (L&N) Railroad 46, 53

M

Manning, Ambrose 11
Marion, Virginia 86, 87, 88
Maynard, Horace 14, 15, 18, 46
   military aid to East Tennessee 32, 42
Mayo, Anna McCarthy. *See* Ingerton, Anna
McCall, Robert B. 71
   character of 72
   death of 71
McClellan, David 26
   arrests bridge burners 35
   Carter County rebellion 31
   Confederate troops 31
McClellan, George B. 25, 31, 32
   and East Tennessee 31, 32
McClellan, Oliver
   death of 48
McKinley, William
   speech honoring East Tennessee 117
McQueen, Samuel 39, 40, 104
   captured 104
   death of 104
   prisoner 104
Miller, Colonel John K. 14, 44, 48, 71, 72, 82
   administering oaths of amnesty 111, 112, 113

INDEX

and Alexander H. Stephens 106
and Andrew Johnson 59, 111
and death of John Hunt Morgan 67
and discipline 51
and Dr. George Thompson 57
and Jimmy Leedy 64
and Patterson's factory 92
and prisoners of war 98
and the Third Brigade 90, 92, 93
and vouchers 110
appeal for advance on Greeneville, Tennessee 64
assisted Major Avery 100
assumes responsibility for Greeneville raid 65
at Salisbury 98
attack at Greeneville, Tennessee 65
at Wytheville, Virginia 94
commissioning a regiment 43
conscription of horses 57
controversy with Major Doughty 82
court-martial of 111
crossing the New River 93
efforts to reduce disease in camp 52
fight at Greeneville, Tennessee 67
grants leave to men 72
leading troops into battle 60
losses at Bulls Gap 74
march to Greeneville, Tennessee 65
personal loss 109, 110
placed under arrest 110
postwar life 123
praise for 60, 62, 98, 110, 111, 123
prisoners of war 100
replacing Lieutenant Colonel Ingerton 81
sheriff of Carter County 43, 100
Stoneman's raid 94, 98, 106
wounded in battle 60, 72
Morgan, John H. 16, 46, 57, 61, 62, 65, 66, 68, 82, 85
and Andrew Campbell 132
burial 132
controversy over death 68, 69, 119, 122
death 66, 67, 71

death defining moment for regiment 119
dismissed notion of surrender 66
in Greeneville, Tennessee 65
inquiry into last Kentucky raid 62
monument 130
myth of 68, 121, 130
prison escape 61
reaction to death 68
reputation 61
school textbook account of death 122
veterans respond to charges of murder 121, 123
Morgan, Richard
brother to John H. Morgan 85
Morristown, Tennessee 62, 72, 73, 76, 91
battle of 73
Mountain Home 129
Mulican, Eli W. 39

N

Nelson, David M.
son of Thomas A.R. Nelson 81
Nelson, Thomas A.R. 14, 18, 20, 21
quote about emancipation 15
slave owner 15
Ninth Tennessee Union Cavalry 65, 66, 75
Northington, Hector 20
Northington, Samuel 19, 20, 22, 23

P

Palmer, Colonel William J.
and Asheville, North Carolina 103
brevetted general 103
First Brigade commander 90, 92, 98, 103, 106, 111
pursuit of Jefferson Davis 104, 105, 106
thoughts about East Tennessee soldiers 106
thoughts about Salisbury Prison 98
Parker, William 39, 40, 41

Index

Payne, William H.
  death of 79
  prisoner at Danville, Virginia 79
  son of Zebulon Payne 79
Payne, Zebulon
  father of William H. Payne 79
Peoples, Madison T. 34, 112
  asks for martial law in East Tennessee 34
  Daniel Ellis remarks about 112
  indicted for treason 112
  oath of allegiance 112
Peoples, William
  father of Madison T. Peoples 112
Pickens, Samuel
  arrest 35

R

Rogers, James T.
  member of John H. Morgan staff 66, 69
Rogersville, Tennessee 19, 60, 62, 85

S

Salisbury, North Carolina 94, 95, 96, 97, 98
Salisbury Prison 84, 92, 98, 100, 109
Saltville, Virginia 62, 85, 88
Sargent, Mattie. *See* Ingerton, Mattie
Schofield, General John M.
  and George Stoneman 84, 90
  commander of Army of the Ohio 80, 83
Scott, Samuel 108, 127
  dishonorable acts of soldiers 106
  elected regimenal historian 129
  failing health 129
  postwar activities 118
  regimental history 8, 14, 106, 119, 129
  trapped behind enemy lines 75
  treated at Mountain Home 129
  veterans' reunions 118
  views of slavery 54

Seddon, James A. 62, 76
Self, Harrison
  pardon 33
Seward, William 25
Sherman, William T. 59, 79, 90, 102, 103
  remarks about Tennessee troops 59
slavery
  abolition and 15
  in East Tennessee 13, 15
  institution of 13
  views of soldiers on 54
Smith, Hamilton C.
  arrested for making incendiary speeches 36
  released on bond 36
Sneed, William H. 18, 121
soldiers' monument 129
Stacy, Brazilliah P. (B.P.) 85, 88, 93, 94, 95, 108
  and Alexander Stephens 106
  and discipline 105
  at Saltville, Virginia 88
  controversy over promotion 82
  death of 128
  declining health 128
  friendship with Samuel Angel 128
  military background 81
  personal background 81
  postwar life 128
  praise of 88, 98
  promotion to lieutenant colonel 81, 82
  recommended by General Samuel P. Carter 82
Stanton, Edwin 44, 45, 46, 47, 84
Stephens, Alexander H. 106
  arrest 107
Stoneman, George 79, 80, 83, 84, 85, 90, 93, 94, 95, 100
  accomplished objectives 98
  and Alvan C. Gillem 90, 92
  and court-martial of Colonel John K. Miller 110
  angry at troops 92
  at Salisbury, North Carolina 94, 97

burning of Salisbury Prison 98
conduct of soldiers 89
conscription of horses 109
exchanged 79
food distributed to poor 97
General Grant's opinion of 84
in Statesville, North Carolina 98
objectives to raid 83, 84
organizing raid 83
preparing for second raid 90
prisoner 79
protection of citizens' property 97
raid into Southwest Virginia 87, 88, 89
report to General Thomas 98
return to Knoxville, Tennessee 98
ruthless warfare carried out by soldiers 90
unwell 98
use of term Cossack 90
Stoneman's raid 11, 84, 104, 111
Stover, Daniel 25, 26, 27, 35, 36
Strawberry Plains, Tennessee 31, 48, 62
Swan, William G. 18

T

Taylor, Andrew D. 26
Taylor, David
  arrested as bridge burner 36
Taylor, George 113
Taylor, Henry 113
Taylor, Nat 113
Taylor, Nathaniel G. 19, 31, 113
Taylorsville, Tennessee 19, 94, 104
Taylor, William 26
Temple, Oliver P. 14, 18
Thirteenth Tennessee Cavalry Association 8, 117, 119, 122, 129
Thomas, George H. 30, 31, 32
Tipton, Eldridge 42
  held hostage by Heatherly gang 42
  released 42
Tipton, Isaac P. 41, 113
  father of Robert and Eldrige Tipton 113
  petition for amnesty 113
Tipton, Robert 41, 42, 114
  death of 42
Trigg, Connally 18
Turkeytown 26

V

Vaughn, John C. 62, 72, 73, 74, 85, 86
Vaughn's Brigade 72, 73
Vaught, Amanda E.
  Confederate sympathizer 114
  widow's pension 116
  wife of George W. Vaught 114
Vaught, George W. 114
  hiding from conscription officers 114
  killed in action 114
  pension 116
Vaught, John H. 40
  death of 40
veterans' reunion 7, 117, 126
Virginia and Tennessee (V&T) Railroad 83, 88, 98

W

Wagner, Joseph 20, 22, 86
Walker, Joshua H. 81, 126, 127
  and William H. Ingerton 80, 126
  arrest of 81
  court-martial of 80
  death of 126
  escape from jail 81
Walker, Leroy P. 23
Watauga Academy 118
Watauga Association 12
Watauga County, North Carolina 11, 91, 100
  records destroyed 92
Watauga River 12, 26, 72, 73
Watauga River Bridge 25, 26, 27, 31
Waugh, Bill 39, 40
  death of 40
Whig Party 13, 35

INDEX

Wilcox, Christopher C. 51, 65, 85
 and John H. Morgan 66, 69, 122
 responds to charges of murder of
  John H. Morgan 121
Williams, Dr. Alexander 64
Williams Home
 John H. Morgan body returned to 67
Williams, Lucy Rumbough
 daughter-in-law of Mrs. Catherine
  Williams 68
Williams, Major William 69
 member of John H. Morgan's staff
  69
 son of Mrs. Catherine Williams 69
 supported John H. Morgan murder
  accusation 69
Williams, Mrs. Catherine 65, 66, 68,
  121
 wife of Dr. Alexander Williams 64
Witcher, Vincent A. 39, 112
Withers, Major Charles A.
 controversy over John H. Morgan's
  death 68, 69
 recounts last moments of John H.
  Morgan's life 68
 urged Morgan to surrender 68
 viewing Morgan's body 69
Wyatt, James B. 57, 58, 86
 accused of destroying private
  property 57
 appeal to Governor Johnson 58
 death of 86
Wytheville, Virginia 35, 73, 83, 87, 93,
  94

Z

Zollicoffer, Felix K. 22, 23, 24, 34

About the Author

A scholar and teacher of American history for more than twenty years, Melanie Storie is a graduate of East Tennessee State University. In 1991, she earned her master's of arts degree in history, and for the past ten years, she has had the pleasure of teaching for her alma mater. In addition to teaching survey courses in U.S. history, she has also taught Tennessee history and women's history. While she enjoys researching, writing and teaching about many historical topics, her main research interest centers on nineteenth-century U.S. history, with a special emphasis on the American Civil War. She lives in Elizabethton, Tennessee, with her husband and two children.

Visit us at
www.historypress.net

This title is also available as an e-book

www.ingramcontent.com/pod-product-compliance
Lightning Source LLC
Chambersburg PA
CBHW042142160426
43201CB00022B/2383